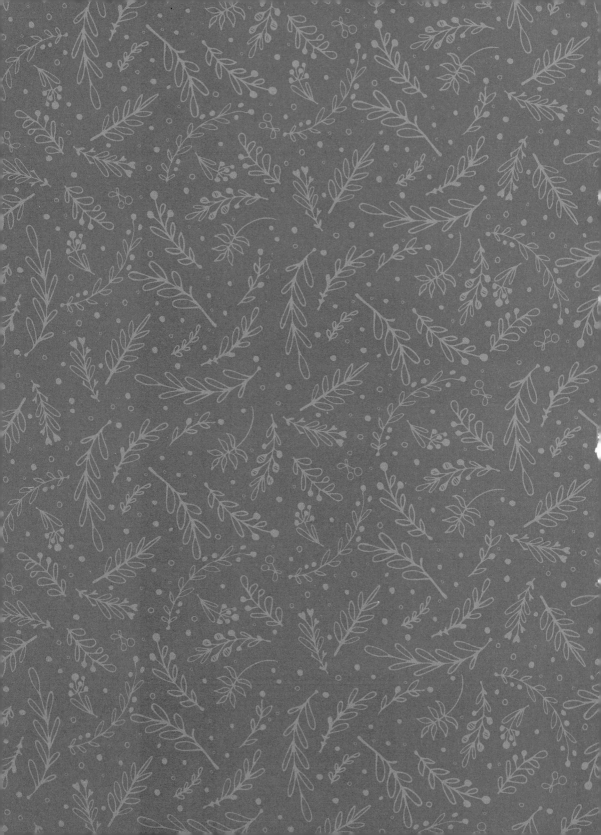

THE OLD FARMER'S ALMANAC

FIELD TO FORK

SELLERS
PUBLISHING

Dedication

To farmers and gardeners across the land, without whose
fertile fields and plots our forks would be empty.

Published by Sellers Publishing, Inc.

161 John Roberts Road, South Portland, ME 04106
Visit us at www.sellerspublishing.com • E-mail: rsp@rsvp.com

© 2018 Sellers Publishing, Inc.
Text © Yankee Publishing Incorporated
Managing Editor: Mary L. Baldwin
Production Editor: Charlotte Cromwell
Editorial assistance: *The Old Farmer's Almanac*
All rights reserved.

ISBN-13: 978-1-4162-4664-0

Printed and bound in China.

10 9 8 7 6 5 4 3 2 1

Credits on page 192.

Contents

Introduction

Since its founding in 1792, *The Old Farmer's Almanac* has been valued by farmers and gardeners for the best advice on growing fruit and vegetables, harvesting and storing them, and using fresh produce in flavorful and nutritious dishes. Almanac readers have long loved its recipes!

Freshness continues to be important to us all, and in these pages you'll find some of our best recipes for bringing great taste and good health to the home table.

From Apple Cranberry Crisp to Savory Zucchini Cakes, these tried-and-true Almanac favorites will help you to use produce at its peak of flavor and turn each season into a celebration of special dishes.

We'd love to hear from you. If you have comments or suggestions about *Field to Fork*, please let us know at Almanac.com/Feedback. Enjoy!

The Almanac Editors

Spring Recipes

Spring arrives with the promise of a fresh start, which is especially true in the garden. Many of the vegetables from our farms and gardens are annuals, which means that every spring we get a do-over. We can ponder new varieties of seeds and seedlings and vow to better prepare the soil and keep the weeds at bay. Luckily, just as we're finishing off the harvest from the root cellar and beginning to put in the hard work to prepare and plant new crops, a handful of delightful spring edibles are popping up to encourage our efforts. Things are off to a sweet start when strawberries and rhubarb meet up in the kitchen. Crunchy radishes, tender lettuce leaves, bright green peas, snappy asparagus, and more are all welcome sights and tastes to usher in a new year in the garden.

Strawberry Crunch Muffins

These muffins are a delight for breakfast or an afternoon snack. Strawberry season is fleeting, but if you can find local, fresh-picked strawberries, you'll be amazed by the juicy, velvety texture and heavenly flavor.

TOPPING:

½ cup brown sugar

¼ cup all-purpose flour

½ cup chopped pecans

¼ cup old-fashioned oats

3 tablespoons unsalted butter, melted

MUFFINS:

¾ cup all-purpose flour

¾ cup whole wheat flour

½ cup sugar

2 teaspoons baking powder

1 teaspoon ground cinnamon

¼ teaspoon salt

1 egg, lightly beaten

½ cup (1 stick) unsalted butter, melted

½ cup milk

1 teaspoon vanilla extract

1 cup sliced strawberries

1 teaspoon grated lemon zest

For topping: In a bowl, combine all topping ingredients and mix well. Set aside.

For muffins: Preheat oven to 350°F. Line cups of a standard muffin tin with paper liners or mist with nonstick cooking spray.

In a bowl, sift together flours, sugar, baking powder, cinnamon, and salt.

In a separate bowl, mix egg, butter, milk, and vanilla. Add wet ingredients to dry ingredients and stir until just combined. Add strawberries and lemon zest and stir just until incorporated; do not overmix. Pour batter into prepared muffin cups, filling them two-thirds full. Sprinkle topping evenly over muffins. Bake for 20 to 25 minutes, or until a toothpick inserted into the center of a muffin comes out clean.

Makes 12 muffins.

 FUN FACT: Strawberries purchased from a supermarket often are tart and have a grainy texture. This is because the natural sugar in the berries begins converting to starch as soon as they are plucked from the plant. If the berries are not ripe when picked and then travel long distances, they scarcely resemble the true fresh fruit by the time they reach the market. It is well worth your effort to find local strawberries or grow your own.

Arugula and Blood Orange Salad

This salad is stunning when made with deep-red blood oranges,
but you can substitute regular oranges if that's what you have available.
If peppery arugula is not to your taste, you can use baby spinach.

2 tablespoons finely chopped shallots

1½ tablespoons balsamic vinegar

3 blood oranges

3 tablespoons extra-virgin olive oil

salt and freshly ground black pepper,
    to taste

3 cups arugula

2 tablespoons toasted pine nuts

4 ounces crumbled Gorgonzola

 FUN FACT: Shallots are a mild-flavored member of the onion family whose seeds can be planted in early spring. There are red, yellow, and white varieties.

In a bowl, combine shallots and vinegar and let sit for at least 20 minutes. Meanwhile, grate the zest of 1 orange, then add zest to shallots. Juice the orange to get ⅓ cup juice, then add juice to shallots. Add olive oil in a thin, steady stream, whisking until dressing is well combined. Taste and season with salt and pepper.

Peel remaining oranges, removing as much of the bitter white pith as possible. Then use a sharp paring knife to cut out the fleshy segments.

Place arugula in a separate bowl, then toss with just enough dressing to coat. Divide arugula among four to six plates. Arrange orange slices over greens, then sprinkle with pine nuts and Gorgonzola. Drizzle with a little more dressing and serve immediately.

Makes 4 to 6 servings.

Minted Peas Salad

Lime juice and fresh mint give a refreshing taste to this salad of chilled fresh peas. Also known as Bibb or Boston lettuce, butter lettuce is the perfect mild lettuce for this salad.

2 pounds shelled fresh peas

1 cucumber, peeled, seeded, and diced

2 tablespoons butter

3 tablespoons chopped fresh mint

1 tablespoon chopped fresh chives

2 tablespoons fresh lime juice

salt and freshly ground black pepper, to taste

1 head butter lettuce, chilled

In a saucepan over medium heat, combine peas, cucumber, butter, and ½ cup of water. Bring to a simmer, cover, and cook for 8 minutes, or until peas are crisp-tender. Drain and transfer to a bowl. While peas are still hot, stir in mint and chives. Cover bowl with plastic wrap and refrigerate.

Just before serving, stir lime juice into pea mixture and season with salt and pepper. Spoon pea salad onto chilled lettuce leaves to serve.

Makes 4 servings.

HARVEST TIPS:
• Pick peas from your garden frequently and regularly to encourage more pods to develop.

• Pick peas in the morning after the dew has evaporated, as this is when they are crispiest.

• Always use two hands when picking peas. Secure the vine with one hand and pull off the peas with your other hand.

Spinach-Strawberry Salad

This salad is a winning combination of strawberries and spinach tossed with a crunchy, sweet-and-sour, poppy-seed dressing. It goes over big, even with those who aren't usually fans of salad. It's bright and pretty, too—perfect for a quick lunch or supper or a small party.

DRESSING:

½ cup sugar

½ cup vegetable oil

¼ cup apple-cider vinegar

2 tablespoons sesame seeds

1 tablespoon poppy seeds

1½ teaspoons minced onion

¼ teaspoon Worcestershire sauce

¼ teaspoon paprika

SALAD:

10 ounces fresh spinach

1 pint strawberries, thinly sliced

walnuts or almonds, optional

For dressing: In a blender, combine all ingredients. Blend well. If dressing seems thick, add a few drops of water.

For salad: Remove stems from spinach and tear leaves into bite-size pieces. Arrange spinach on individual plates or in a serving bowl. Arrange strawberries and nuts (if using) on top of spinach. Drizzle dressing over salad and serve.

Makes 4 to 6 servings.

FUN FACTS: Spinach is higher in iron, calcium, and vitamins than most cultivated greens, and it's one of the best sources of vitamins A, B, and C.

Stir-Fried Radishes With Scallions

Thinly sliced radishes are paired with scallions and cooked lightly, then finished with melted butter for a quick and crunchy side dish or perfect partner for grilled meat.

3 tablespoons vegetable oil

2 bunches red radishes, thinly sliced

4 scallions, sliced

salt and freshly ground black pepper, to taste

2 tablespoons butter, cut into chunks

HARVEST TIPS:
• Some varieties of radish are ready to harvest as soon as 3 weeks after planting.

• Do not leave radishes in the ground long after they mature; their condition will deteriorate quickly.

• Cut the tops off short, wash the radishes, and dry them thoroughly. Refrigerate in plastic bags. Radish greens can be refrigerated separately for up to 3 days.

In a wok or skillet over high heat, warm oil. Add radishes and toss to coat. Stir for 30 seconds, then add scallions. Sprinkle 3 tablespoons of water over radishes and continue stirring until water evaporates and radishes are crisp-tender. Remove from heat. Season with salt and pepper, then add butter. Toss until butter is melted and serve immediately.

Makes 4 servings.

Cilantro and Mint Sauce

This is a wonderfully tasty and useful sauce to have in your recipe repertoire.
Pair it with fish or lamb or serve it as a dip with cruciferous vegetables.

½ cup plain yogurt

1 or 2 spring onions, diced

1 or 2 jalapeños, seeded and diced

½ cup fresh cilantro leaves

½ cup fresh mint leaves

salt and freshly ground black pepper,
    to taste

In a blender or food processor, combine yogurt, onions, peppers, cilantro, and mint. Process, scraping down sides every 15 seconds, for 1 minute, or until ingredients are finely chopped and mixture is smooth. Season with salt and pepper.

Makes ¾ cup.

HARVEST TIPS:
• Frequent harvesting is the key to keeping mint plants at their best. Young leaves have more flavor than old ones, and mint can be harvested as soon as it comes up in spring.

• Right before a mint plant flowers, cut the stems 1 inch from the ground. You can harvest one mint plant two or three times in one growing season. You can also just pick the leaves as you need them.

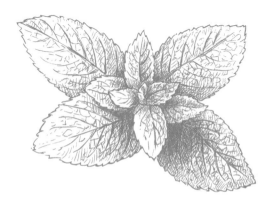

Asparagus Salad With Mustard Vinaigrette

Because asparagus is a perennial, it's often one of the first spring signs that the garden has come back to life. This salad showcases this harbinger of early garden goodness.

2 pounds fresh asparagus, trimmed

MUSTARD VINAIGRETTE:

¼ cup balsamic, champagne, or red-wine vinegar

2 to 3 teaspoons Dijon-style mustard

2 to 3 teaspoons brown sugar

1 clove garlic, minced

¾ cup olive oil

½ teaspoon salt, or to taste

freshly ground black pepper, to taste

SALAD:

4 handfuls fresh baby spinach

handful fresh Italian parsley

salt and freshly ground black pepper, to taste

1 hard-boiled egg, finely chopped

1 cup herb-flavored croutons (whole, if small; otherwise, partially crushed)

fresh Parmesan cheese shavings (optional)

For asparagus: Put two dinner plates in the freezer. Lay asparagus in a steamer basket. Add ½ inch of water to a pot and bring to a boil. Carefully put basket into pot, cover, and steam for 3 minutes, or until spears are bright green in color. (Pencil-thin spears cook quickly; thumb-thick ones require 1 to 2 minutes more. Avoid wilting the spears.)

Remove plates from freezer and immediately transfer asparagus onto them, spreading spears so that they do not overlap. Set aside to cool, or cover and refrigerate for 1 to 2 hours before serving.

For Mustard Vinaigrette: In a bowl, combine vinegar, mustard, brown sugar, and garlic. Whisk to dissolve sugar. While whisking, add olive oil in a slow, steady stream. Season with salt and pepper and continue to whisk. Taste and adjust seasonings as needed.

For salad: Mix spinach and parsley and arrange in a bed on a platter. Season with salt and pepper. Lay asparagus spears over greens, drizzle with ¼ cup of vinaigrette, and top with egg, croutons, and Parmesan (if using). Pass remaining vinaigrette at the table.

Makes 6 servings.

Variations:

Tomato Vinaigrette: Whisk 1 tablespoon tomato paste into Mustard Vinaigrette after adding the olive oil. Taste and adjust seasonings with a pinch of brown sugar, if desired.

Herb Vinaigrette: Add up to 1 tablespoon chopped fresh basil or ¾ teaspoon dried basil, oregano, or thyme to Mustard Vinaigrette when adding salt and pepper.

Asparagus With Orange Sauce

This flavor combination is a nice change of pace for asparagus in season.

2 teaspoons fresh lemon juice

6 tablespoons fresh orange juice, divided

2 teaspoons grated orange zest

½ teaspoon salt

freshly ground black pepper, to taste

3 egg yolks

6 tablespoons (¾ stick) unsalted butter, melted

2 pounds fresh asparagus, trimmed

In a saucepan over medium heat, combine 2 tablespoons of water, lemon juice, 4 tablespoons orange juice, orange zest, salt, and pepper. Heat, stirring occasionally, until liquid is reduced to 3 to 4 tablespoons. Reduce heat to low and add egg yolks one at a time, whisking continuously until sauce is very thick. Remove from heat and slowly drizzle in butter, whisking constantly. Slowly add remaining 2 tablespoons of orange juice, a little at a time. Strain sauce to remove zest, if desired. Keep sauce warm over a pan of warm water while asparagus cooks.

Lay asparagus in a steamer basket. Add ½ inch of water to a large pot and bring to a boil. Carefully put basket into pot, cover, and steam for 3 minutes, or until spears are bright green in color. (Pencil-thin spears cook quickly; thumb-thick ones require 1 to 2 minutes more. Avoid wilting the spears.)

When asparagus is ready, place sauce in a warmed ceramic bowl and serve, with a ladle, alongside the asparagus.

Makes 4 to 6 servings.

Cooking Variation:
Another great way to cook fresh asparagus is to roast it in the oven. Preheat oven to 400°F. Spread asparagus in a single layer on a baking sheet and drizzle with olive oil (about 2 tablespoons per pound of asparagus). Season with salt and pepper, then toss to coat. Bake for 15 minutes, or until tender.

Lemony Asparagus and Spring Pea Salad With Roasted Almonds

This refreshing and nutritious salad is loaded with spring vegetables. Use thin, tender asparagus so that it won't overwhelm the peas in flavor or texture.

⅓ cup plus 3 tablespoons extra-virgin olive oil

¼ cup minced shallots

⅓ cup whole almonds

2 tablespoons fresh lemon juice

1 pound asparagus, trimmed

¾ cup shelled fresh peas

2 teaspoons grated lemon zest

3 sprigs fresh mint, stems removed

kosher or sea salt and ground white pepper, to taste

4 ounces Parmigiano-Reggiano cheese, shaved, for garnish

 FUN FACT: White asparagus is not a variety, but simply asparagus grown in the absence of sunlight to prevent chlorophyll from developing. White asparagus is slightly sweeter than green asparagus but has less fiber.

In a skillet over medium heat, warm ⅓ cup of oil. Add shallots and cook for about 5 minutes, or until translucent. Scrape shallots and oil from skillet into a bowl and set aside. Add 3 tablespoons of oil to same skillet over medium heat. Once oil is shimmering, add almonds and toast for 6 to 8 minutes, stirring frequently, until lightly browned. Add almonds to shallot mixture. Stir in lemon juice and set aside.

Prepare an ice-water bath and set aside. In a pot over high heat, bring 4 cups of salted water to a boil. Add asparagus and return water to a boil; cook for 3 to 4 minutes. Remove asparagus (reserving water in pot) and place in ice-water bath. Return reserved water to a boil and blanch peas for 3 minutes, or until soft. Drain peas and refresh under cold running water. Add peas to bowl with shallots. Drain asparagus and pat dry.

Arrange asparagus spears on a serving platter with tips all facing the same direction. Add lemon zest and mint leaves to bowl with shallots and season with salt and pepper. Liberally spoon over asparagus and garnish with Parmigiano-Reggiano shavings.

Makes 6 servings.

Asparagus Frittata

A frittata is a wonderful way to make a few special ingredients go a long way. If your asparagus patch is young and you don't have a lot to harvest yet, this is the perfect way to feature this spring vegetable without needing large bunches of asparagus.

9 spears pencil-thin asparagus, trimmed and cut into ¾-inch lengths

3 tablespoons olive oil

1 red onion, cut into ¼-inch-thick slices

pinch of sugar

¾ teaspoon kosher or sea salt

6 eggs

¾ cup coarsely grated Parmigiano-Reggiano cheese

½ teaspoon freshly ground black pepper

Prepare an ice-water bath and set aside. Bring a pot of salted water to a boil, add asparagus, and cook for 3 to 4 minutes. Drain asparagus and submerge in ice-water bath. Drain and set aside.

In an ovenproof skillet over medium heat, warm olive oil. Add onions, sugar, and salt; reduce heat to medium-low and cook, stirring occasionally, for about 30 minutes, or until onions are golden brown and very tender. Remove onions from the pan, leaving as much oil in pan as possible. Let onions cool for 10 minutes.

In a bowl, whisk eggs until smooth. Add Parmigiano-Reggiano, pepper, asparagus, and onions. Set skillet with oil over medium heat. Add egg mixture, stirring briefly to distribute fillings. Reduce heat to low and let mixture cook slowly; you should see just a few bubbles popping up around the edges. Cook undisturbed for 8 minutes, or until edges are set but middle is still very liquid. Meanwhile, set oven broiler on high.

Transfer skillet to oven and position 3 to 4 inches below broiler. Cook for about 2 minutes, until top of frittata is golden brown, edges are puffed, and center is just set. Don't overcook it! Remove from oven, loosen edges with a spatula, then transfer to a platter and serve immediately.

Makes 4 servings.

Herby Bulgur Salad

This healthy, filling dish is packed with fresh flavors and whole grain.
Bulgur boasts more nutrients and fiber than other grains and offers a subtle
nutty flavor and light texture—what more could you ask for in a meal?

1 cup bulgur

¾ cup chopped dried cherries
    or cranberries

¾ cup chopped pecans

¾ cup chopped fresh parsley

¾ cup chopped fresh chives

¾ cup chopped fresh mint

½ cup fresh lemon juice

1 teaspoon sugar

½ cup extra-virgin olive oil

Put bulgur into a bowl and just cover it with boiling water. Set aside for 2 hours or until all liquid is absorbed. Mix in cherries, pecans, parsley, chives, and mint.

In a separate bowl or jar with a lid, combine lemon juice and sugar. Stir or shake until the sugar dissolves. Slowly add oil and stir to incorporate.

Immediately before serving, pour dressing over salad and stir to coat.

Makes 6 servings.

 FUN FACT: Bulgur is a Middle Eastern staple grain derived from whole durum wheat berries that have been steamed, roasted, and crushed.

Dandelion Pesto

Dandelion pesto is a classic pesto recipe with the addition of wild spring dandelion greens. Harvest dandelion greens when they are young; the longer they grow, the more bitter their flavor becomes. Note: It is important to forage dandelion greens from areas that have not been sprayed with pesticides or other chemicals.

2 cups tightly packed dandelion leaves, well rinsed and dried

1 dozen large basil leaves

2 cloves garlic

1 cup toasted hazelnuts, almonds, pine nuts, or walnuts, skins removed

½ cup extra-virgin olive oil

½ cup grated Parmigiano-Reggiano cheese (optional)

kosher or sea salt and freshly ground black pepper, to taste

FUN FACT: If you consider dandelions a pesky weed, maybe their nutritional value will change your mind: Dandelion greens are a great source of dietary fiber; vitamins A, B_6, C, E, and K; thiamin; riboflavin; calcium; iron; potassium; and manganese. Plus, they're free!

In a blender or food processor, pulse dandelion leaves, basil, garlic, and nuts. Scrape down sides of bowl to make sure that all ingredients are combined. With the motor running, add oil and process until a smooth paste forms. Add Parmigiano-Reggiano (if using). Season to taste with salt and pepper. Serve with pasta, as a pizza topping, or however you typically use pesto.

Makes 3½ cups.

Rosemary Chicken With Garlicky Spinach

If you have garlic scapes (the flower stalks of the garlic plant) or green garlic, you can use either of these in place of garlic cloves.

4 chicken breast halves, with skin

salt and freshly ground black pepper, to taste

2 cloves garlic, 1 finely chopped and 1 thinly sliced

1 tablespoon chopped fresh rosemary

3 tablespoons olive oil, divided

3 tablespoons red-wine vinegar, divided

1 pound fresh spinach, stems removed

½ teaspoon sugar

 FUN FACT: Garlic scapes are the tops (looped flower stalks) of hardneck garlic. Trimming the scapes will encourage the plants to put all of their energy into bulb formation. Plus, garlic scapes already contain that potent garlic flavor and can be used in any dish where you would use garlic cloves. Pop them into a blender with olive oil and Parmesan cheese to make pesto. Or, stir-fry them as you would green beans, but just don't add too much additional spice.

Place chicken breasts on a plate and season with salt and pepper. Sprinkle with chopped garlic and rosemary, turning once or twice to coat evenly.

In a bowl, whisk together 2 tablespoons oil and 1 tablespoon vinegar. Pour over chicken and set aside to marinate for 20 to 30 minutes. Meanwhile, steam spinach until barely wilted.

In a heavy skillet over medium-high heat, place chicken breasts, skin side down. Reduce heat to medium and cook for 8 minutes, or until browned. Turn chicken over, cover pan, and cook for 5 minutes. Remove cover and continue cooking for 3 minutes, or until chicken is cooked through. An instant-read thermometer inserted into the thickest part of the breast should read 165°F.

Place a separate skillet over medium heat. Combine remaining 1 tablespoon oil and sliced garlic and heat just until garlic sizzles. Remove skillet from heat, add spinach, and toss to coat.

Remove chicken from skillet. Add sugar and remaining 2 tablespoons vinegar to skillet and boil, stirring, for about 1 minute, until mixture is blended and reduced by half. Drizzle a little of this glaze over each chicken breast. Serve on a bed of spinach.

Makes 4 servings.

Cream of Fiddleheads Soup

Early spring means fiddleheads—the young, tightly curled fronds of the ostrich fern. If you aren't a forager or friend of a forager, you can sometimes find fiddleheads at markets during the short window when they are in season. If you can't find fiddleheads, you can make this soup with sliced fresh asparagus.

1½ cups fiddleheads, cleaned and finely chopped

2 tablespoons butter

2 cubes chicken bouillon or 2 teaspoons chicken bouillon granules

1 onion, minced

1 clove garlic, minced

2 cups milk

2 cups heavy cream

salt and freshly ground black pepper, to taste

Put fiddleheads into a steamer basket. Add ½ inch of water to a pot and bring to a boil. Carefully put basket into pot, cover, and steam for 10 to 12 minutes, or until tender.

In a saucepan over medium heat, melt butter with bouillon. Add fiddleheads, onions, and garlic and cook for 10 minutes. Add milk, stirring frequently, until everything is heated thoroughly. Add cream, stir to incorporate, then season with salt and pepper. Serve hot.

Makes 6 servings.

 FUN FACT: Ferns are an ancient family of plants that first showed up in fossil records from a time over 100 million years before dinosaurs walked upon Earth. In fact, ferns grew before flowering plants existed.

Red Radish Soup

Cooked and puréed radishes create a surprisingly mellow soup. Be sure to leave the red peel on the radishes so that the soup will have a delicate pink blush.

3 tablespoons butter

3 scallions (white part only), sliced

6 cups chicken broth

2 bunches red radishes, quartered

¼ cup long-grain rice

1 tablespoon fresh lemon juice

1 teaspoon finely chopped fresh
     ginger

½ cup plain yogurt

finely chopped fresh parsley,
     for garnish

In a saucepan over medium heat, melt butter. Add scallions and toss to coat evenly. Continue stirring until scallions are tender. Pour in chicken broth, then add radishes and rice. Cover and simmer for 20 minutes, or until radishes and rice are tender. Remove from heat and cool slightly.

Pour soup into a blender or food processor and process until smooth, then return to saucepan. Stir in lemon juice and ginger, then blend in yogurt. Cook over low heat and warm gently, but do not allow soup to boil. Garnish with parsley before serving.

Makes 6 servings.

Spring Lamb Stew

This stew is a celebration of the young, new vegetables coming up in the garden and in markets—small new potatoes, spring onions, baby carrots, and tiny tender peas.

4 tablespoons (½ stick) butter

3 pounds boned lamb shoulder, cut into 1-inch cubes

2 tablespoons all-purpose flour

3 sprigs fresh parsley

1 sprig fresh rosemary

1 fresh bay leaf

1 clove garlic, minced

½ cup dry white wine

3 cups beef stock

12 small, whole new potatoes

12 baby carrots, peeled

12 small, whole white onions

1 cup shelled fresh peas

salt and freshly ground black pepper, to taste

Preheat oven to 325°F. Get out a Dutch oven.

In a skillet over low heat, melt butter. Add lamb and brown on all sides. Put browned meat into Dutch oven and warm over low heat. Sprinkle flour over lamb and stir gently until blended. Add parsley, rosemary, bay leaf, and garlic. Add wine and stock, stirring to form a smooth sauce. Cover Dutch oven and place in oven for 1 hour.

Add potatoes, carrots, and onions to Dutch oven (make sure that there is ample liquid to cover all vegetables; add water if necessary) and return to oven to cook for 30 minutes longer.

Place peas in a saucepan, add ½ cup of boiling water, and simmer, covered, for 5 minutes. (Don't cook peas any longer, or they will lose their bright green color.) Drain, add to stew, season with salt and pepper, and serve.

Makes 4 to 6 servings.

Grilled Pizza With Spiced Lamb, Feta, and Arugula

While lamb meat is available year-round, it is really at its tastiest in the late spring. Seek a local source for lamb or at least a skilled and knowledgeable butcher who can give you information on how and where the lamb was raised.

Pizza Dough (recipe on page 186)

½ pound ground lamb

4 tablespoons extra-virgin olive oil, divided

1 onion, finely chopped

1 clove garlic, minced

2 teaspoons ground cumin

2 teaspoons finely chopped fresh oregano

4 cups arugula

2 tablespoons fresh lemon juice

kosher or sea salt and freshly ground black pepper, to taste

1 cup crumbled feta cheese

Follow directions on page 186 to prepare dough, dividing it into four equal balls for final rise. (Smaller pizza crusts are easier to work with on a grill.)

In a skillet over medium-high heat, cook lamb in 1 tablespoon of oil, breaking up meat with a wooden spoon. When lamb is cooked through, use a slotted spoon to remove it to a plate. Set aside to cool.

Wipe skillet clean and place over medium heat. Add 1 tablespoon of oil and cook onions and garlic until softened and translucent. Stir in cumin and oregano, then cook for 1 minute to release fragrance. Remove from heat and let cool. Add lamb to skillet and mix well.

In a bowl, combine arugula, lemon juice, and remaining 2 tablespoons of oil. Season to taste with salt and pepper and toss to combine. Heat a grill to medium-high and lightly oil the grates.

Roll out each ball of dough as thin as possible. Place two dough rounds on grates and cook for about 1 minute, or until very lightly browned. Turn dough over and immediately sprinkle with a portion of lamb mixture and feta. Cover grill and cook pizzas for about 2 minutes, or until edges of crusts have browned. When done, remove pizzas from grill and repeat process with remaining dough rounds. Spoon arugula mixture evenly over the tops of pizzas before serving.

Makes 6 servings.

Sorrel Linguine With Spring Peas, Green Garlic, and Fresh Ricotta

Making linguine from scratch with fresh herbs takes a bit of work (pasta machine recommended), but you'll be amazed at how delicious it is. This dish also takes well to the addition of fresh crabmeat, lobster, or shrimp.

1 bunch fresh sorrel,
plus 3 tablespoons
chopped fresh sorrel

1 egg

1 cup all-purpose flour,
plus extra for dusting

½ cup semolina

¼ cup cold water

¼ cup extra-virgin olive oil

1 sprig green garlic, chopped

1 cup shelled fresh peas

¼ cup grated Parmigiano-Reggiano
cheese

3 tablespoons finely chopped
fresh mint

2 tablespoons chopped fresh chives
(reserve blossoms for garnish)

2 tablespoons unsalted butter

1 tablespoon fresh lemon juice

kosher or sea salt and freshly ground
black pepper, to taste

1 cup fresh ricotta cheese,
at room temperature

In a blender or food processor, purée the bunch of sorrel with the egg.

In a bowl, combine flour and semolina. Make a well in the center and pour in puréed sorrel. Mix until a ball begins to form. Add cold water, a little at a time, until dough comes together. Flour dough lightly, then feed through a pasta machine's widest opening. Repeat, decreasing the opening one increment at a time, until the next-to-last setting (or the last setting if you prefer your pasta thinner). You may have to cut the length of pasta as the sheets get longer and longer with each pass through the machine.

Roll fresh sheets of pasta into a scroll and cut into ¼-inch-wide pieces. Unroll each cut piece, and you'll have linguine noodles. Cover pasta with a towel until ready to cook. (You may make the pasta a day ahead. Just place it on a lightly floured baking sheet, cover, and refrigerate.)

Bring a pot of salted water to a boil. In a large skillet over medium heat, warm oil and cook garlic gently. Add pasta and peas to boiling water and cook for 2 to 3 minutes, or until al dente. Drain and add pasta and peas to pan with garlic. Add Parmigiano-Reggiano, mint, chives, butter, and chopped sorrel; toss to combine. Add lemon juice and season with salt and pepper. Divide among four warm bowls and top with ricotta and chive blossoms.

Makes 4 servings.

Rhubarb Coffee Cake

What better way to start the morning than with a steaming mug of coffee and a generous piece of tangy rhubarb coffee cake with cinnamon-sugar topping? Or, if you prefer your sweets later in the day, serve this for an afternoon snack or dessert.

CAKE:

2 cups all-purpose flour

1 teaspoon baking soda

½ teaspoon salt

½ cup (1 stick) unsalted butter, softened

1½ cups brown sugar

1 egg

1 cup sour cream

2½ cups fresh rhubarb, cut into ½-inch chunks

1 teaspoon vanilla extract

TOPPING:

½ cup sugar

½ cup chopped pecans or walnuts

1 tablespoon butter, melted

1 teaspoon ground cinnamon

For cake: Preheat oven to 350°F. Grease and flour a 13x9-inch baking dish.

In a bowl, whisk together flour, baking soda, and salt.

In a separate bowl, cream together butter and brown sugar for 4 to 6 minutes, or until fluffy. Beat in egg. Add one-third of the flour mixture and stir gently. Add half of the sour cream and stir. Repeat with flour mixture, remaining sour cream, and remaining flour mixture. Stir in rhubarb and vanilla, then spread batter into prepared baking dish.

For topping: In a bowl, combine sugar, pecans, butter, and cinnamon. Sprinkle over top of cake.

Bake for 40 to 50 minutes, or until a toothpick inserted into the center comes out clean.

Makes 12 servings.

Rhubarb Sauce

This deep-pink sauce is lovely-looking and -tasting atop vanilla ice cream, spooned over pound cake, stirred into warm oatmeal, and in myriad other ways. If you're blessed with armloads of rhubarb stalks, consider canning some of this sauce to give as homemade gifts.

2 scant cups sugar

3 pounds rhubarb, cut into 1-inch pieces to make about 9 cups

HARVEST TIPS:
• Do not harvest rhubarb stalks during the first growing season. This will allow the plants a full growing season to become established.

• Harvest rhubarb stalks when they are 12 to 18 inches long.

• To pick rhubarb, grab the base of the stalk and pull it away from the plant with a gentle twist. If this doesn't work, use a sharp knife to cut the stalk at the base.

• Always leave at least two stalks per plant to ensure continued production. If grown in the right conditions and treated well, rhubarb plants may offer a bountiful harvest for up to 20 years.

In a saucepan over medium heat, combine 2 cups of water and the sugar. Bring to a boil, stirring frequently. Once syrup has boiled for a few minutes and is fully bubbling in the center, add rhubarb. Watch closely for sauce to return to a full boil, then boil for 1 minute more. Remove from heat and immediately pour into a bowl or pan with a tight cover. Leave tightly covered until cold.

Makes 6 to 8 cups.

Strawberry-Chocolate Pie

Here's a strawberry-chocolate pie that requires no baking and just six ingredients besides the crust! For best taste, enjoy this elegant and light dessert on the same day that you make it.

6 ounces (¾ package) cream cheese, softened

1 teaspoon vanilla extract

¾ cup heavy cream, at room temperature

½ cup sugar

9-inch graham cracker crust

2 cups hulled and halved strawberries

2 squares (2 ounces total) bittersweet chocolate, melted

 FUN FACT: Although strawberry plants will produce fruit in their first year, it's best to pick off blossoms to discourage fruiting. If you keep them from bearing fruit in their first spring, they will use their food reserves to develop healthy roots—and your second-year strawberry yield will be much greater than otherwise.

In a bowl, beat cream cheese and vanilla until blended and light. Set aside.

Using an electric hand or stand mixer and a chilled bowl, whip the cream until doubled in volume. Continue beating on high speed while adding sugar a little at a time. Add cream cheese mixture and beat briefly, just until combined.

Pour mixture into piecrust, arrange strawberries on top, and drizzle with melted chocolate. Refrigerate, uncovered, for at least 4 hours before serving.

Makes 6 to 8 servings.

Grilled Angel Food Cake With Berry Wine Sauce and Lemon Whipped Cream

This recipe requires the freshest of strawberries, so seek out a U-Pick strawberry farm or find a good local source. This is also a great excuse to fire up the grill, and you won't believe how impressive and delightful a grilled slice of airy cake can taste.

SAUCE:

1 cup sugar

1 cup good cabernet wine

1 cinnamon stick

orange rind stuck with 4 cloves

2 pounds strawberries, hulled
    and sliced

WHIPPED CREAM:

1 cup heavy cream

3 tablespoons confectioners' sugar

1 tablespoon grated lemon zest

1 tablespoon fresh lemon juice

1 teaspoon vanilla extract

CAKE:

1 prepared angel food cake, sliced

sliced strawberries, for garnish

fresh mint sprigs, for garnish

For sauce: In a saucepan, combine sugar, wine, cinnamon stick, and orange rind with cloves. Bring to a boil and simmer for 30 minutes, or until reduced by half, stirring occasionally. Strain over a bowl and discard cinnamon stick, orange rind, and cloves. Set aside to cool.

Once sauce has cooled, add strawberries and stir to coat. Chill sauce in refrigerator.

For whipped cream: Using an electric hand or stand mixer, beat heavy cream until foamy. Gradually add confectioners' sugar, lemon zest, lemon juice, and vanilla. Continue whipping until soft peaks form. Set aside.

To assemble: Preheat grill to medium. Spray angel food cake slices with cooking spray. Grill cake slices on each side for 2 to 3 minutes, or until grill marks appear and slices are golden brown. Place each cake slice on a serving dish. Spoon strawberry sauce over cake and top with a dollop of whipped cream. Garnish with sliced strawberries and mint.

Makes 8 servings.

Lemon Soufflé Pancakes

These fluffy, lemony pancakes are the ultimate breakfast or brunch food.
Look for fresh, juicy, organic lemons to use for juicing and zesting.

3 eggs, separated

1 cup cottage cheese

½ cup all-purpose flour

2 tablespoons vegetable oil

2 tablespoons fresh lemon juice

2 tablespoons grated lemon zest

1 tablespoon maple syrup,
    plus more for serving

2 teaspoons baking powder

¼ teaspoon salt

Grease and preheat a griddle over high heat.

In a bowl, beat egg whites until stiff; set aside.

In a blender or food processor, combine egg yolks, cottage cheese, flour, oil, lemon juice, lemon zest, maple syrup, baking powder, and salt and blend until smooth. Pour batter into a separate bowl and gently fold in egg whites.

Pour batter onto griddle and cook for about 3 to 4 minutes per side. Serve with warm maple syrup.

Makes 6 servings.

Strawberry Shortcake

When fresh berries abound, who can resist the charm of this classic dessert?
Let the sliced, sugared berries sit for at least an hour to get good and juicy.

2 pounds fresh strawberries, sliced

½ cup confectioners' sugar

SHORTBREAD:
2 cups all-purpose flour

4 teaspoons baking powder

1 tablespoon sugar

½ teaspoon salt

5 tablespoons cold, unsalted butter

¾ cup milk

WHIPPED CREAM:
1 cup heavy cream

1 tablespoon sugar

1 teaspoon vanilla extract

In a bowl, combine strawberries with confectioners' sugar and toss gently. Set aside.

For shortbread: Preheat oven to 425°F. Butter base and sides of a 9-inch pie plate.

In a bowl, whisk together flour, baking powder, sugar, and salt. Using a pastry cutter or two forks, cut butter into flour mixture until it resembles coarse crumbs. Make a well in the center and add milk, stirring with a fork just to blend.

Gather dough in your hands and knead it twice on a floured work surface. Press dough into pie plate and bake for 15 minutes, or until lightly browned. Cool slightly.

For whipped cream: Using an electric hand or stand mixer, whip cream with sugar and vanilla until medium-size peaks form. Refrigerate if not using right away.

To assemble: Cut shortbread into wedges. Split each wedge and spoon sweetened berries over one half of shortbread wedges. Place the other half of shortbread wedges over berries, then top with more sweetened berries and whipped cream.

Makes 6 to 8 servings.

Strawberry-Rhubarb Soup

This special blend of flavors works as well in soup as it does in pie.
You can serve this soup warm, but we recommend it chilled.

6 cups chopped rhubarb

2 cups hulled and sliced strawberries

2 tablespoons cornstarch

¼ cup cold water or dry white wine

¼ cup sugar, or more to taste

1 cup heavy cream

1 egg yolk

sliced strawberries, for garnish

FUN FACTS:
• Rhubarb is a perennial
vegetable, although it is
generally used as a fruit in
desserts and jams.

* Only the stalks of the rhubarb
plant are eaten; they have a
rich, tart flavor. The leaves are
poisonous, so be sure not to
ingest them.

In a pot over medium-high heat, combine rhubarb, strawberries, and 1½ quarts of water. Partially cover and bring to a simmer, then cook for 20 minutes. Strain, reserving fruit, and return liquid to pot. Reheat to a simmer.

In a bowl, combine cornstarch and cold water to form a smooth paste. Add ½ cup of hot soup to paste, stir with a whisk until blended, then add mixture to pot with soup. Cook over low heat, stirring constantly, until smooth. Add sugar and reserved fruit and stir.

In a separate bowl, combine cream and egg yolk, then stir slowly into soup. Do not boil. Remove soup from heat and let cool. Once cooled, put in refrigerator to chill. Serve cold, garnished with additional sliced strawberries.

Makes 6 to 8 servings.

Summer Recipes

Summer makes eating seasonally and supporting your local farmers a dream. The parade of fresh fruit and vegetables ready for harvest throughout these months is scrumptious, healthy, and inspiring. Much of the summer garden, orchard, and farm bounty is so delicious, it can be consumed in the field, directly off the plant or tree. Berries and stone fruit from U-Pick farms and orchards, still warm from the summer sun, may be too tempting in their fresh and raw form to make it all the way home and into a pie. Fresh peas and carrots and tomatoes are perfect for summer snacking without any prep work at all. Luckily, the abundance of fresh food from the field allows for plenty of cooking creativity, too. The summer recipes in this chapter take full advantage of the sweet and savory bonanza that awaits throughout this most satisfying season.

Peach, Red Onion, and Tomato Salsa

This salsa recipe is wonderful for peach season, and all of its main ingredients are usually available at the same time at farmers' markets. Make a big batch and enjoy with tortilla chips, tacos, quesadillas, or any other meal that goes well with traditional salsa.

1½ cups finely diced fresh, ripe peaches

1½ cups cored, seeded, and finely diced tomatoes

½ cup finely chopped red onion

½ cup finely chopped bell pepper

1 to 2 tablespoons fresh lime juice

¼ cup chopped pickled jalapeños, plus 1 teaspoon juice

1 tablespoon chopped fresh basil

1 tablespoon chopped fresh Italian parsley

2 to 3 teaspoons sugar

salt, to taste

In a bowl, combine all of the ingredients. Refrigerate for several hours. Stir and taste occasionally, adjusting the seasoning as needed.

Transfer to one or more jars with a lid, cover, and refrigerate for up to a week.

Makes about 4 cups.

FUN FACTS: Although peaches are native to the Chinese countryside, the peach was brought to the Western world from Iran. Peach trees can grow in USDA Zones 5 to 8 but do especially well in Zones 6 and 7. There are standard-size and dwarf peach tree varieties, plus most types are self-fertile, so even peach lovers with only a small space can grow their own fruit crop.

Savory Zucchini Cakes

Enjoy these zucchini cakes alone or on a bun with lettuce and tomato. These tasty, savory cakes are yet another wonderful way to make good use of a bountiful zucchini harvest.

3 medium zucchini

1½ cups bread crumbs

2 eggs, beaten

2 tablespoons mayonnaise

1½ teaspoons Old Bay seasoning

1 teaspoon spicy brown mustard

1 onion, finely chopped

1 green or red bell pepper, finely chopped

salt and freshly ground black pepper, to taste

2 tablespoons olive oil

tartar sauce, for serving

 FUN FACT: Zucchini are loaded with vitamins and minerals. They have more potassium than bananas!

Shred zucchini into a colander over a bowl. Let drain for 30 to 45 minutes. Press down to remove excess water and pat dry with a paper towel.

In a bowl, combine zucchini, bread crumbs, eggs, mayonnaise, Old Bay, mustard, onions, bell peppers, and salt and pepper.

Using an ice cream scoop, place a portion of the mixture in your hand, form it into a ball, and press down lightly to form a cake. Repeat with the rest of the mixture.

In a nonstick skillet over medium-low heat, warm oil. Gently transfer cakes to the skillet using a spatula. Don't crowd the pan. Turn cakes every minute until they are golden brown and crispy on both sides. Add more olive oil for subsequent batches if the pan gets dry. Drain on paper towels and serve hot with tartar sauce.

Makes about 20 cakes.

Warm Nectarine and Prosciutto Antipasto

Pairing the warm, sweet taste of nectarines with salty prosciutto makes a wonderful first course.

4 ripe nectarines or 6 fresh apricots

¼ cup extra-virgin olive oil

12 slices prosciutto

fresh thyme sprigs, for garnish

FUN FACT: Peaches and nectarines are the same fruit and share the same scientific name, *Prunus persica*. Their only difference lies in one gene that controls the fuzz. Whether you enjoy them fuzzy or clean-shaven, you will agree that there is nothing like the taste and aroma of these fruit when eaten straight from the tree.

Position oven rack on top shelf and preheat broiler. Get out a baking sheet.

Cut nectarines into quarters (if using apricots, cut in half) and remove pits. Dip cut side of fruit in olive oil and place, cut side up, on baking sheet. Place fruit under broiler for 3 to 5 minutes.

While fruit is still warm but not too hot to touch, plate nectarines and arrange prosciutto slices atop cut sides of fruit. Serve warm, garnished with thyme.

Makes 4 servings.

Basil Pesto

Fresh pesto has become a favorite sauce for many. It's delicious served over steaming pasta, used as a pizza topping, or spread on fresh bread. This recipe calls for basil, but you can experiment with other herbs such as parsley, thyme, tarragon, and cilantro. If you're a fan of garlic, feel free to use more.

3 cloves garlic

2 cups fresh basil leaves

¼ cup pine nuts or walnuts

1½ teaspoons salt

¼ teaspoon pepper

½ cup extra-virgin olive oil

3 ounces Parmesan cheese, grated

In a blender or food processor, combine garlic, basil, nuts, salt, pepper, and half of the oil. Purée, then slowly add remaining oil. If using immediately, stir in Parmesan; if not, freeze mixture in a resealable plastic bag, squeezing out any air. (Pesto turns brown when exposed to air.) Add Parmesan before serving.

Makes 1½ cups.

FUN FACTS: Basil is one of the earliest known herbs and is surrounded by fascinating folklore from many regions: It has been associated with both love and madness! The early Romans thought that it caused insanity. Ancient Greeks believed that to have a successful basil crop, you had to shout and swear at the seeds while planting. In Europe, lovers exchanged sprigs of basil as a symbol of faithfulness. In rural Mexico, basil is thought to have the power to return a lover's roving eye. In Haiti, it was used by the pagan love goddess Erzulie as a protector. Shopkeepers there sprinkle basil water around their stores to ward off evil spirits and bring prosperity.

Grilled Corn and Watermelon Relish

You'll likely find ripe watermelon and freshly picked corn at farmers' markets at around the same time, and this sweet and crunchy relish brings these two summer highlights together. It's perfect served with grilled striped bass or other mild-flavored white-meat fish.

4 tablespoons extra-virgin olive oil, divided

6 ears corn, husked

sea salt and freshly ground black pepper, to taste

1 small seedless watermelon (about 2 pounds), cut into 2-inch-thick slices, rind removed

½ cup maple syrup

2 cloves garlic, minced

1 red onion, diced

¼ cup chopped fresh cilantro

zest and juice of 1 lemon

zest and juice of 1 lime

HARVEST TIPS:
• Watermelons don't sweeten after they are picked, so be sure to wait until fully ripe to harvest.

• Watermelons can be stored uncut for about 10 days. If cut, they can last in the refrigerator for about 4 days if wrapped tightly in plastic wrap.

Preheat grill to medium-high.

Rub 3 tablespoons olive oil over corn and season with salt and pepper. Place on grill and cook for 8 to 10 minutes, turning frequently. Add watermelon to grill and cook for 1 to 2 minutes on each side. Remove corn and watermelon from grill and set aside to cool. Once cooled, cut corn kernels off cobs and dice watermelon into ½-inch cubes.

In a saucepan on the grill or stove top, heat maple syrup until bubbling. Add watermelon and stir to combine. Remove from heat and set aside.

In a bowl, combine corn, garlic, onions, cilantro, zest and juice of lemon and lime, remaining 1 tablespoon of olive oil, and maple syrup and watermelon. Season to taste with salt and pepper.

Makes about 4 cups.

Lemon Zucchini Muffins

Shredded fresh zucchini doesn't alter the flavor of these lemony muffins, but it does give them a moister texture and a nutritional boost.

2 cups all-purpose flour

½ cup sugar

1 tablespoon baking powder

2 teaspoons freshly grated lemon zest

½ teaspoon salt

¼ teaspoon ground nutmeg

½ cup chopped walnuts

½ cup raisins

2 eggs

½ cup milk

⅓ cup vegetable oil

1 cup packed shredded zucchini

FUN FACT: The main difference between winter and summer squash varieties is their harvest time; the shorter growing period gives summer squash a thin, edible skin.

Preheat oven to 400°F. Line cups of a standard muffin tin with paper liners or mist with nonstick cooking spray.

In a bowl, whisk together flour, sugar, baking powder, lemon zest, salt, and nutmeg. Stir in nuts and raisins.

In a separate bowl, beat eggs, then beat in milk and oil. Add to flour mixture, then add zucchini and stir until just blended. Fill muffin cups. Bake for 20 to 24 minutes, or until a toothpick inserted into the center comes out clean and the tops are golden brown.

Makes 12 muffins.

Farmers' Market Grilled Veggie Platter

Almost any vegetable can be grilled, and this basic recipe adapts well to whatever is ready to harvest when you plan to fire up the grill. The vegetables listed below are only a starting point, so experiment with your favorites.

4 pounds mixed fresh, seasonal vegetables suitable for grilling (such as summer squash, onions, fennel, eggplant, carrots, corn, peppers, portobello mushrooms)

2 cups vegetable oil

1 cup apple cider vinegar

1 cup spicy mustard

dried herbs, to taste (such as oregano, sage, thyme, basil)

FUN FACT: The common green and red bell peppers that we see in supermarkets are actually the same thing; the red peppers have just been allowed to mature on the plant longer, changing color and also producing a larger amount of vitamin C.

Clean, trim, and peel vegetables. Slice larger ones (such as squash and eggplant) into ¼-inch-thick pieces. You can grill many vegetables whole or cut them into wide strips or slices for skewering. Skewer small vegetables and onions. Place vegetables in two extra-large, resealable plastic bags. Combine remaining ingredients and divide between the two bags. Refrigerate until ready to use.

Preheat grill to medium-low heat. Remove vegetables from bags and shake off excess marinade. Place vegetables on grill, staggering them by size and density. Grill carrots, fennel, peppers, and onions for 20 to 25 minutes. Grill eggplant slices for 10 minutes. Grill corn sections for 15 to 20 minutes. Grill summer squash and portobello mushrooms for 5 to 7 minutes. Turn vegetables partway through their grilling time for consistent cooking. The vegetables should be tender but not burned. Arrange grilled vegetables on a large platter to make a colorful side dish.

Makes 8 to 10 servings.

Panzanella

This bread, tomato, and cucumber salad is a perfect expression of a summer garden in a bowl. Be sure to harvest or select slicing cucumbers that aren't too large—about 6 to 8 inches—or they may taste bitter.

6 tomatoes, cored and cut
    into small wedges

2 cucumbers (preferably seedless),
    sliced into half-moons

1 red onion, thinly sliced

8 basil leaves, torn

¼ cup extra-virgin olive oil

1 tablespoon red-wine vinegar

kosher or sea salt, to taste

1 small loaf Italian bread,
    cut in a ¾-inch dice and toasted

In a bowl, combine tomatoes, cucumbers, onions, basil, oil, vinegar, and salt. Let sit at room temperature for 30 minutes. Taste and add more salt, if desired. Mix in bread and serve.

Makes 6 servings.

HARVEST TIPS:
• At peak harvesting time, you should pick cucumbers every couple of days. They grow quickly!

• Any cucumbers left on the vine too long will get tough skins and lower plant productivity.

• Cucumbers will keep for a week to 10 days when stored properly in the refrigerator.

Sweet Refrigerator Pickles

If you have a bumper crop of cucumbers, this is a good way to quickly preserve them without heating up the kitchen.

6 to 8 medium cucumbers, sliced
   (approximately 8 cups)

2 onions, sliced

2 bell peppers, sliced

3 hot peppers, sliced

1 tablespoon salt

2 cups sugar

2 cups apple cider vinegar

2 teaspoons celery seeds

2 teaspoons mustard seeds

 FUN FACTS: The phrase "cool as a cucumber" first appeared in "A New Song of New Similes" by John Gay (1685–1732), in a simile suggesting its renown as a cooling agent. This is probably because cucumbers contain 96 percent water, more than any other fruit or vegetable.

In a bowl, combine cucumbers, onions, and peppers. Sprinkle with salt and set aside for 1 hour. Drain liquid.

In a separate bowl, stir together sugar, vinegar, celery seeds, and mustard seeds until sugar is dissolved. Pour over cucumbers and stir. Store in a large glass or plastic covered container in the refrigerator.

These can be eaten right away, but the flavor is better after about 1 week. They will keep for 1 to 2 months in the refrigerator.

Makes about 10 cups.

Classic Gazpacho

This quintessential summer soup has been a tradition in Spain for centuries.
With all of the fresh flavor and nutrients of raw vegetables,
it has aptly been called a liquid salad.

3 pounds tomatoes, diced

1 onion, diced

1 large or 2 small green bell peppers,
    diced

1 clove garlic, minced

½ cup extra-virgin olive oil

2 tablespoons sherry vinegar
    or other vinegar

1 slice white bread, crust cut off,
    saturated with cold water

¼ cup chopped fresh cilantro

¼ cup chopped fresh parsley

½ tablespoon hot pepper sauce

2 teaspoons salt, or to taste

In a blender or food processor, purée tomatoes, onions, and peppers (each separately) until smooth.

In a bowl, combine processed vegetables and remaining ingredients and stir to blend. Set aside for 30 minutes to an hour to allow flavors to marry. Serve cold.

Makes 6 servings.

FUN FACT: In 1893, the United States Supreme Court ruled that since tomatoes are most often served during the main part of the meal, either alone or with vegetables, they are vegetables. However, biologically speaking, tomatoes are actually fruit.

White Radish Salad

Shredded white radishes, carrots, and zucchini combine to create a
tasty and attractive slaw. The flavor of the white radish is milder than
that of the more common red radish. Chill this salad and serve
with baked ham or corned beef.

1 bunch white radishes, trimmed

2 carrots

1 small zucchini

salt and freshly ground black pepper,
    to taste

2 tablespoons white-wine vinegar

½ teaspoon ground mustard

1 teaspoon dried oregano

6 tablespoons olive oil

2 ounces Gorgonzola cheese,
    finely crumbled

By hand or using a food processor, shred radishes,
carrots, and zucchini and combine in a bowl. Season with
salt and pepper and toss to combine.

In a separate bowl, whisk together vinegar and mustard
until mustard is dissolved. Stir in oregano. Gradually
whisk in oil. Pour dressing over shredded vegetables
and toss to coat. Cover and refrigerate for 2 to 3 hours, or
until lightly chilled. Just before serving, add Gorgonzola
and toss to incorporate.

Makes 4 servings.

PLANTING TIP:
Let the radishes do
the work! Radish
seeds are natural
companions to
carrots. Mix radish seeds
with carrot seeds before
you sow, especially if your
soil tends to develop a
tough crust. Radish sprouts
will push up through the soil
first, breaking it up for the
later-sprouting carrots. As
you harvest the radishes,
the carrots will fill in the
row.

Green Beans Vinaigrette

These lovely tiny bundles ("tied" with pimento strips) are marvelous to take along on a picnic. Select or harvest green beans that are crunchy but tender and not too large. Overly mature beans will be stringy, tough, and less than ideal in this or any other recipe.

½ cup dry white wine

¼ cup olive oil

½ teaspoon dried thyme

½ teaspoon salt

¼ teaspoon fennel seeds

12 black peppercorns

1 bay leaf

3 scallions, sliced

2 sprigs fresh parsley

2 strips (1 inch each) lemon zest

½ cup chopped celery leaves

1 pound whole green beans

2 tablespoons fresh lemon juice

1 teaspoon dried tarragon

2 pimentos, cut into narrow strips

In a wide saucepan, combine wine, oil, and 3 cups of water. Stir in thyme, salt, fennel seeds, peppercorns, and bay leaf. Add scallions, parsley, lemon zest, and celery leaves and bring to a boil.

Drop beans into the boiling liquid and cook, uncovered, for 6 to 8 minutes, or until crisp-tender. Lift beans out with a slotted spoon and place in a deep rectangular dish. Continue to boil liquid until it is reduced by half. Stir in lemon juice and tarragon, then pour over beans. Cover dish with wax paper, then with aluminum foil. Refrigerate for 24 hours.

Remove beans from the liquid and divide into eight small portions, lining them up like bundles of sticks. Wind a narrow strip of pimento around each bundle and overlap the ends. Serve immediately or, if packing for a picnic, enclose each bundle in a piece of plastic wrap.

Makes 8 servings.

Fresh Tomato and Zucchini au Gratin

This dish is perfect for those years when you have a bumper crop of tomatoes and zucchini, which is a common occurrence in even a simple vegetable garden. Draining the tomatoes keeps the dish from getting watery.

4 tomatoes, cored

salt, to taste, plus ¼ teaspoon

3 medium zucchini

⅓ cup heavy cream (optional)

1 large slice dense white or whole wheat bread, cut into cubes

½ cup finely grated Parmesan cheese

small handful fresh Italian parsley

2 teaspoons dried basil or 6 to 7 leaves fresh basil, finely chopped

¼ teaspoon freshly ground black pepper

3 tablespoons olive oil

HARVEST TIPS:
• Never place tomatoes on a sunny windowsill to ripen; they may rot before they are ripe!

• If your tomato plant still has fruit when the first hard frost threatens, pull up the entire plant and hang it upside down in the basement or garage. Pick tomatoes as they redden.

• Never refrigerate fresh tomatoes. Doing so spoils the flavor and texture that make up that garden tomato taste.

Cut tomatoes into ¼-inch-thick slices. Place slices in a colander over a bowl. Salt, to taste, and toss to coat. Set aside to drain for 30 minutes.

Rinse and dry zucchini. Slice each one into ¼-inch-thick slices, cutting slightly on the diagonal. Put slices into a bowl, salt, to taste, and toss lightly. Set aside for 15 to 20 minutes.

Preheat oven to 400°F. Butter a shallow 13x9-inch baking dish or large gratin dish. (For a slightly richer version, if using the heavy cream, pour it into the dish and tilt to coat.)

In a food processor, combine bread, Parmesan, and parsley. Pulse to reduce bread to fine crumbs. Transfer to a bowl and add basil, ¼ teaspoon salt, and pepper. Mix to blend.

Lay zucchini slices on paper towels and pat dry. Lay tomato slices in the bottom of the prepared baking dish. Place zucchini slices on top. Spread bread crumbs over zucchini and evenly drizzle oil on top. Bake for about 30 minutes, or until bubbly.

Makes 6 servings.

Grilled Baby Vegetables With Garlic-Saffron Butter

Baby zucchini squash are becoming more popular at farmers' markets, and they make a gorgeous presentation. You can also make this recipe with regular zucchini and summer squash: Simply cut squash into half-moon shapes about ½-inch thick and cook directly on your grill (no need to parcook ahead of time).

GARLIC–SAFFRON BUTTER:

½ cup dry white wine
(such as pinot grigio)

¼ teaspoon saffron threads

2 tablespoons olive oil

1 clove garlic, minced

1 cup (2 sticks) unsalted butter,
softened

1½ teaspoons minced fresh parsley

½ teaspoon kosher or sea salt

½ teaspoon freshly ground
black pepper

VEGETABLES:

2 tablespoons salt, plus extra
for vegetables

1 pound baby carrots

1 pound whole baby zucchini

1 pound whole baby pattypan squash

olive oil

freshly ground black pepper

 FUN FACT: Garlic is easy to grow and produces numerous bulbs after a long growing season. It adds wonderful flavor to many dishes and can be used raw, roasted, sautéed, or even pickled. Beyond its intense flavor and culinary uses, "the stinking rose" is good in the garden as an insect repellent.

For Garlic-Saffron Butter: In a saucepan over medium-high heat, warm wine for 4 to 5 minutes, or until just steaming. Pour into a heatproof cup; sprinkle saffron threads over top and stir. Set aside.

Return saucepan to heat; add oil and garlic. Cook, stirring, until garlic is translucent, 3 to 4 minutes. Pour saffron-wine mix back into pan and whisk together; then set aside to cool.

Using an electric hand or stand mixer, beat butter, parsley, salt, and pepper at medium speed until blended. Gradually add in wine mixture, beating until liquid is incorporated. Chill in an airtight container for at least 40 minutes, or until firm.

For vegetables: Bring a pot of water to a boil over high heat. Add salt, then add carrots, zucchini, and squash; cook for 3 to 4 minutes, or until crisp-tender (carrots may need an additional few minutes, depending on thickness). Drain. Plunge vegetables into ice water to stop cooking and drain again.

Submerge 12 wooden skewers in water and let soak for 10 minutes. Meanwhile, preheat grill for direct medium heat.

Thread vegetables onto skewers. Brush with oil and sprinkle lightly with salt and pepper. Grill vegetables for 4 to 5 minutes on each side, or to desired doneness. Serve warm with Garlic–Saffron Butter.

Makes 8 to 10 servings.

Green Bean and Basil Soup

Puréed green beans and fresh basil combine to form a compelling and sophisticated soup. Select green beans at their peak: They should have vivid color and a firm texture that delivers a satisfying "snap" when broken.

3 tablespoons butter

2 leeks, thinly sliced

1 clove garlic, minced

4 cups chicken broth

2 mealy potatoes (such as russets),
    peeled and cut into cubes

1 pound green beans,
    cut into 1-inch lengths

½ cup fresh basil leaves,
    coarsely chopped

½ cup heavy cream

1 tablespoon chopped fresh savory

1 tablespoon fresh lemon juice

½ teaspoon salt

pinch of cayenne pepper

sliced mushrooms, for garnish

In a saucepan over medium heat, melt butter. Add leeks and garlic and toss to coat. Cook until leeks are tender. Add chicken broth, potatoes, and green beans. Bring to a gentle boil. Cover pan and cook for 20 minutes, or until potatoes and green beans are tender. Stir in basil and cook, uncovered, for 5 minutes.

Pour contents of pan into a blender or food processor and process until smooth. Return to pan and stir. Add cream, savory, lemon juice, salt, and cayenne. Warm gently, but do not allow soup to boil. Ladle into bowls and garnish with mushrooms.

Makes 6 servings.

FUN FACT: What makes some potato varieties mealy and others waxy? It's all about the ratio of starch, moisture, and sugar in the potato. Mealy potatoes have a higher starch content but a low sugar and moisture content. They fall apart easily, which make them a great addition to creamy, blended soups. Waxy potatoes have a low starch content and a high sugar and moisture content, so they hold their shape well during cooking, making them ideal for roasting or sautéing.

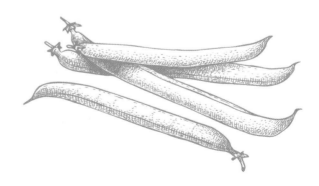

Ratatouille-Poached Eggs

Loaded with summer vegetables, this old favorite is new again when served with poached eggs. The addition of eggs also adds a blast of protein to turn this into a healthful one-dish meal.

¼ cup olive oil

1 onion, finely chopped

1 medium zucchini, cut in a ¼-inch dice

2 cups peeled, finely diced eggplant

2 cloves garlic, minced

½ teaspoon paprika

2 cups finely diced plum tomatoes

salt and freshly ground black pepper, to taste

balsamic vinegar, to taste

8 teaspoons Basil Pesto (recipe on page 48)

4 eggs

chopped fresh parsley, for garnish

chopped pitted olives, for garnish

In a large, nonreactive skillet, warm oil over medium heat. Add onions and cook for 5 minutes, or until soft. Add zucchini and eggplant and cook for 3 to 4 minutes more, or until soft. Add garlic and paprika and cook for 1 minute. Add tomatoes and bring to a simmer. Add salt, pepper, and balsamic vinegar, and simmer for 7 to 8 minutes.

With the back of a large spoon, make four depressions in the ratatouille. Drop 2 teaspoons of pesto into each. One at a time, crack each egg into a small bowl, then slide the egg into a depression in the ratatouille. Cover skillet and cook for 4 to 6 minutes, or until eggs are done to your liking. Garnish with parsley and olives before serving.

Makes 4 servings.

FUN FACT: Did you know that you can tell what color eggs a hen will lay by the color of her ear? Birds don't have external ears like humans do, so look for a small circle or oval of skin on the side of the head, next to the ear hole. If it's white, your hen will lay white eggs; if it's red, she'll lay brown ones. Egg color does not affect flavor or nutrition.

Eggplant Hoagies

This eggplant hoagie is the perfect summer sandwich. If you have an abundance of cucumbers and tomatoes, make extra Cucumber Salad—it's good enough to eat on its own.

CUCUMBER SALAD:

1½ cups peeled, seeded, and finely diced cucumbers

1½ cups seeded, chopped plum tomatoes

¼ cup chopped fresh parsley

½ red onion, chopped

salt and freshly ground black pepper, to taste

TAHINI SAUCE:

¼ cup tahini paste

1 tablespoon fresh lemon juice

SANDWICHES:

1 pound eggplant, peeled and sliced into ½-inch rounds

kosher salt

peanut oil for frying

4 small hoagie or French rolls

1 cup hummus

4 hard-boiled eggs, sliced

For Cucumber Salad: In a bowl, combine cucumbers, tomatoes, parsley, onions, and salt and pepper. Set aside.

For Tahini Sauce: Whisk together tahini paste, lemon juice, and 3 tablespoons of water. Add more water and lemon juice, as necessary, to achieve desired consistency. Set aside.

For sandwiches: Sprinkle eggplant with salt on both sides, place on a baking sheet or wire rack, and set aside for 30 minutes. Brush off salt and press eggplant slices firmly between paper towels to remove excess moisture.

In a skillet, heat 1 inch of oil to 375°F, or very hot but not smoking. Working in batches, fry eggplant slices for 5 to 6 minutes on one side and 2 to 3 minutes on the other, or until brown and tender. Using a slotted spoon, transfer eggplant to paper towels to drain and cool.

Split hoagie rolls almost in half lengthwise. Spread 2 tablespoons of hummus on each side. Divide sliced eggs, eggplant, and Cucumber Salad equally among the four rolls. Drizzle each with 2 tablespoons Tahini Sauce.

Makes 4 sandwiches.

Roasted Red Pepper, Mozzarella, and Basil-Stuffed Chicken

It is perfectly acceptable to use jarred roasted red peppers for this recipe, but it's also possible to roast your own peppers. See instructions in the tip below if you have red peppers to process for this or other recipes.

4 boneless, skinless chicken breast halves

1 tablespoon dried Italian seasoning, divided

salt and freshly ground black pepper, to taste

12 ounces sweet roasted red peppers, sliced into 1-inch pieces

1 bunch fresh basil leaves

8 ounces fresh mozzarella, cut into 8 slices

¼ cup freshly grated Parmesan cheese

 COOKING TIP: To roast red peppers, preheat oven to 450°F. Place whole red peppers on an aluminum foil–lined baking sheet and roast for 20 to 25 minutes. Peppers should be blistered and slightly blackened. Remove from oven, place peppers in a brown paper bag, and fold to seal tightly. Let stand 10 minutes, or until cool. Peel peppers, slice in half, and remove and discard seeds. Cut peppers into wedges and store in a jar in the refrigerator.

Preheat oven to 400°F. Grease a 13x9-inch, broiler-safe casserole.

Butterfly chicken breast halves: Slice through each breast horizontally, leaving a ¼-inch "hinge."

Open chicken breast and place in casserole. Sprinkle with half of Italian seasoning and salt and pepper. On one side (half) of each breast, layer roasted red peppers, basil leaves, and 1 slice mozzarella. Fold over other side, tucking in fillings. Sprinkle with remaining Italian seasoning.

Bake for 30 to 40 minutes, or until internal temperature of chicken breast reaches 165°F on an instant-read thermometer. Remove from oven. Turn oven to broil. Top each breast with 1 slice mozzarella. Sprinkle with Parmesan. Broil until cheese is browned and bubbly, about 5 minutes.

Makes 4 servings.

Corn and Black Bean Pitas

Because fresh sweet corn loses its sweetness soon after harvesting, it should be prepared for eating immediately after picking. The corn's sweet crunch pairs perfectly with creamy black beans in this salad/sandwich combo.

4 ears fresh corn, husked

3 cups or 2 cans (15 ounces each) cooked black beans

1 cup chopped red onion

1 cup diced celery

3 tablespoons balsamic vinegar

1 tablespoon olive oil

2 ounces feta cheese, crumbled

2 pitas (6-inch), warmed

In a pot, boil corn until tender. Cool, then cut kernels from cobs into a bowl. Add black beans, onions, celery, vinegar, oil, and feta and toss well. Cut pitas in half and open the pockets. Spoon filling into pita halves.

Makes 4 servings.

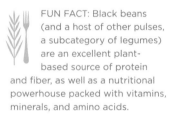

FUN FACT: Black beans (and a host of other pulses, a subcategory of legumes) are an excellent plant-based source of protein and fiber, as well as a nutritional powerhouse packed with vitamins, minerals, and amino acids.

Corn and Chive Polenta Cakes With Salad Greens and Prosciutto

These crispy corn cakes mimic griddle cakes with fried ham, but with a more complex flavor and a little more style. To add a bit of peppery tang to the dish, include mustard, mizuna, broadleaf cress, or arugula in your salad green mix.

CAKES:

2 tablespoons plus ½ cup canola oil, divided

1 cup fresh corn kernels

salt and freshly ground black pepper, to taste

1 cup chicken stock

¾ cup coarse-grain cornmeal

¼ cup (½ stick) salted butter

½ cup grated Parmesan cheese

¼ cup finely chopped chives

½ cup all-purpose flour

SALAD:

2 teaspoons Dijon-style mustard

2 tablespoons fresh lemon juice

1 teaspoon honey

1 teaspoon fresh minced chives

½ teaspoon salt

⅓ cup olive oil

4 cups mixed salad greens

4 ounces (about 8 thin slices) prosciutto, cut lengthwise into strips

Grease a 9x9-inch baking dish.

For cakes: In a pan over medium heat, warm 2 tablespoons of oil. Add corn and cook until just heated through, about 2 to 3 minutes. Remove from heat and season with salt and pepper. Set aside.

In a saucepan, bring 1 cup of water and stock to a boil; then lower heat to a simmer and gradually add cornmeal in a slow, steady stream. Keep over low heat and continue stirring with a wooden spoon for 35 minutes, or until smooth. Stir in butter, sautéed corn, Parmesan, and chives, then season with salt and pepper.

Spread cornmeal mixture to a ¾-inch thickness in prepared pan and refrigerate for at least 1 hour, or until firm.

When cornmeal mixture is set, cut into rounds with a cookie cutter or rim of a clean glass to make eight rounds.

In a skillet, warm remaining ½ cup of oil over high heat. Dip cornmeal rounds into flour, brush off excess, and fry for 2 to 3 minutes per side, or until crisp and golden brown. Drain on paper towels and keep warm.

For salad: In a bowl, whisk together mustard, lemon juice, honey, chives, and salt. Slowly drizzle in olive oil, whisking continuously, until it emulsifies.

Toss salad greens with vinaigrette. Divide among four plates. Place two polenta cakes on each plate and top with prosciutto. Serve warm.

Makes 4 servings.

Zoodles (Zucchini Noodles)

If you find yourself with a couple of large zucchini and you've already eaten and given away more zucchini bread than you can imagine, make zoodles! Zoodles are a fun way to use zucchini and a healthy, fresh alternative to pasta. You can enjoy zoodles lightly sautéed or try this recipe that combines avocados, goat cheese, and pesto into a creamy sauce.

1 to 2 ripe avocados,
    peeled and pitted

2 ounces regular or herbed
    goat cheese

1 to 2 tablespoons Basil Pesto
    (recipe on page 48)

4 to 5 teaspoons olive oil, divided

1 to 2 large zucchini

1 to 2 cloves garlic, minced

grated Parmesan cheese, to taste

FUN FACTS: The world's heaviest zucchini, grown by Bernard Lavery of Plymouth, England, grew 69½ inches long and weighed almost 65 pounds. A Pennsylvania man, Tom Roy, designated August 8 as National Sneak Some Zucchini Onto Your Neighbor's Porch Day. To celebrate it, you simply wait until the dead of night and quietly creep up to your neighbors' front doors, leaving plenty of zucchini for them to enjoy.

In a food processor, combine avocados, goat cheese, pesto, and 1 to 2 teaspoons of oil. Process until combined; mixture will be thick. Set aside.

Using a spiralizer or serrated peeler, twist or peel zucchini into noodles. Process only the firm flesh, not the seeded portion. Set aside.

In a skillet over medium heat, warm 1 tablespoon of oil. Add garlic and cook for 30 seconds. Add zoodles and cook, stirring frequently, for 8 to 10 minutes, or until soft and zoodles have sweated several tablespoons of liquid. Remove from heat. Drain liquid, reserving 1 to 2 tablespoons.

Add avocado mixture to skillet with zoodles and stir to coat. Add reserved zucchini liquid, ½ tablespoon at a time, if desired, to thin avocado mixture. Add Parmesan and stir to blend. Serve, with additional Parmesan to pass at the table.

Makes about 4 servings.

Variations:
• Cook zoodles as directed, but skip the avocado mixture. Instead, top with tomato sauce.

• Cook as directed and add zest and juice of ½ lemon during the last minute of cooking. Remove zoodles from pan, reserving the liquid. Return liquid to pan and add ½ pound raw, peeled, and cleaned shrimp. Cook until shrimp are pink, adding ¼ cup white wine, if desired. Serve shrimp over zoodles, sprinkled with grated Parmesan.

Grilled Chicken With Summer Herbs

For this perfect summer recipe, you can prepare the marinade in the morning and let the chicken breasts marinate for up to 8 hours or otherwise just let them sit for 30 minutes before dinner. Instead of chicken breasts, you may also want to try cubes of chicken or pork to make kabobs.

1 cup loosely packed mixed fresh herb leaves (such as basil, Thai basil, cilantro, mint, parsley), chopped

2 cloves garlic

¼ cup olive oil

¼ cup fresh lemon juice

1 tablespoon kosher or sea salt

¼ teaspoon freshly ground black pepper

4 boneless, skinless chicken breasts halves, patted dry

FUN FACT: The most common type of basil is sweet basil; some other types include purple basil (less sweet than common basil), lemon basil (lemon flavor), and Thai basil (licorice flavor).

In a food processor, combine herbs, garlic, oil, lemon juice, salt, and pepper. Purée until a smooth paste forms. If mixture seems dry and herbs aren't puréeing, add a little more olive oil. Put chicken breasts into a resealable plastic bag, pour in marinade, seal, and massage briefly. Chill for at least 30 minutes or up to 8 hours.

Preheat grill until hot. Grill chicken 10 to 15 minutes on each side, or until an instant-read thermometer inserted into the middle of the breast reads 165°F.

Makes 4 servings.

Mixed Vegetable Frittata

When you have a little of this and a little of that ready to harvest from your garden or leftover vegetables from your trip to the farmers' market, this is your go-to recipe. You can even use whatever cheese you happen to have—from soft, fresh chèvre to hard, salty Parmesan, any type will do.

7 to 9 eggs

splash of milk

olive oil

½ onion, diced

2 to 4 cloves garlic, chopped

½ to ¾ cup chopped vegetables (any combination of fresh vegetables and leafy greens)

salt and freshly ground black pepper, to taste

fresh herbs (optional)

2 handfuls grated, shredded, or crumbled cheese of your choosing

Preheat oven to 350°F. Grease a pie plate or 8x8-inch baking dish.

In a bowl, beat eggs with milk until combined. Set aside.

In a skillet, warm oil over medium heat. Cook onions and garlic for 2 to 3 minutes, or until soft. Add vegetables and cook, stirring, until softened. Season with salt, pepper, and fresh herbs (if using).

Slide the veggies into prepared pie plate, sprinkle cheese on top, and pour eggs evenly over all. Bake for 20 minutes; eggs should be set and firm, but not too dry. Let sit for 10 to 15 minutes before serving. Leftovers can be refrigerated and served cold.

Makes 8 servings.

Fresh Tomato Tart

This fresh tomato tart recipe is a work of art! Use summer's best tomatoes and a free-form pastry. Mmmm!

Food Processor Tart Dough (recipe on page 184), or pie dough of your choice

⅓ cup Basil Pesto (recipe on page 48)

½ cup finely grated Parmesan cheese, divided

1½ tablespoons fine cornmeal

4 to 5 large tomatoes, cored, halved, seeded, and sliced ¼-inch thick

salt and freshly ground black pepper, to taste

¼ cup heavy cream

basil leaves, for garnish

 HARVEST TIP: The best method for storing and preserving basil is freezing. Freezing will prevent the plant from losing any of its flavor. To quick-freeze basil, dry whole sprigs of basil and package them in airtight resealable plastic bags, then place in the freezer.

Preheat oven to 400°F.

On a large sheet of floured parchment paper or wax paper, roll prepared tart dough into a large rectangle slightly less than ¼-inch thick. If you're using parchment paper, slide the paper and pastry onto a large baking sheet and trim the paper so that it fits the pan. If you're using wax paper, invert the pastry onto the pan and peel off the paper. Spread pesto on the pastry, leaving a 1-inch border.

In a bowl, combine ¼ cup of Parmesan and the cornmeal, then sprinkle over the pesto. Layer on tomato slices (about five slices per row). Season with salt and pepper. Fold the edge of the pastry over the perimeter of the tomatoes.

Bake on the center oven rack for 20 minutes. Remove from the oven, sprinkle with remaining Parmesan, and drizzle with cream. Reduce heat to 375°F and bake for 25 to 30 minutes more, or until crust is golden and filling is bubbling. Transfer to a cooling rack for 5 to 10 minutes before serving. Garnish with basil leaves.

Makes 8 servings.

Chicken-Stuffed Tomatoes

These compact, tasty, and satisfying stuffed tomatoes are also impressive-looking on the plate. Select tomatoes that are large enough to have room for ample herby chicken filling.

4 large, firm tomatoes

1½ cups diced cooked chicken

1 cup diced celery

1 tablespoon chopped fresh chervil or 1 teaspoon dried chervil

1 tablespoon chopped fresh basil or 1 teaspoon dried basil

½ tablespoon chopped fresh thyme or ¼ teaspoon dried thyme

3 tablespoons heavy cream

salt and freshly ground black pepper, to taste

butter, to taste

parsley, for garnish

Preheat oven to 350°F. Grease a 9x9-inch baking dish.

Core tomatoes and scoop out seeds, leaving tomato wall at least ¼-inch thick. Place tomatoes in prepared baking dish.

In a bowl, combine chicken, celery, chervil, basil, and thyme and mix well. Add cream and toss until everything is coated. Season with salt and pepper.

Spoon chicken mixture into tomato shells. Dot the top of each tomato with butter and bake for 20 minutes. Garnish with parsley and serve warm.

Makes 4 servings.

FUN FACT: Europeans didn't embrace tomatoes—even calling them "poison apples"—until the invention of the pizza in 1880 by the Italians. Royalty used lead trenchers (a precursor to the plate) for tableware, and the acid of tomatoes sucked up the lead and sickened or killed regal diners. Poor folks used wood trenchers and therefore ate tomatoes with abandon, as they were plentiful and cheap.

Peach-Glazed Chicken With Grilled Peaches

If you have a peach tree or went to a local U-Pick peach orchard, you may have put up some peach preserves that you can use here. If not, store-bought preserves or jam are fine for the glaze. Just be sure to use fresh, ripe peaches on the grill for full flavor.

GLAZE:

2 cups peach preserves or jam

3 tablespoons olive oil

2 tablespoons soy sauce

1 tablespoon Dijon-style mustard

1 tablespoon minced garlic

1 small jalapeño, finely chopped

salt and freshly ground black pepper, to taste

CHICKEN:

8 Frenched (wing bone exposed) chicken breasts

olive oil

salt and freshly ground black pepper, to taste

4 peaches, cut in half and pitted

Preheat grill.

For glaze: In a bowl, combine peach preserves, oil, soy sauce, mustard, garlic, and jalapeño. Season with salt and pepper. Reserve ½ cup of glaze.

For chicken: Brush chicken with oil and season with salt and pepper. Place skin side down on the grill and cook for 6 to 7 minutes, or until golden brown. Turn over chicken and continue cooking for 5 to 6 minutes. Brush both sides with glaze and continue cooking for an additional 4 to 5 minutes.

Place peach halves, cut side down, on the grill and cook for 2 minutes. Turn over and brush with reserved glaze. Cook for 3 to 4 more minutes, or until peaches are soft.

Serve chicken with grilled peaches on the side.

Makes 4 servings.

COOKING TIP: A Frenched chicken breast is also known as "airline chicken" or "chicken supreme." It is a boneless chicken breast with the upper portion of wing bone left on and the bone scraped clean and exposed. This butchering technique is also often applied to lamb or veal.

Plum Crostata

A crostata is a free-form pie or tart that is baked on a baking sheet
instead of in a pie plate. This recipe uses plums, but peaches
and/or nectarines work just as well.

Three-Grain Butter Pastry
  (recipe on page 183)

3½ cups pitted and sliced ripe plums

¼ cup sugar, plus extra for sprinkling

4 teaspoons cornstarch

2 teaspoons fresh lemon juice

1½ tablespoons fine yellow cornmeal
  or semolina

nutmeg, to taste

milk, for glaze

Prepare dough as directed. Lightly butter a large baking sheet. Set aside. Roll dough into a 12½-inch circle and place it on prepared sheet. Put sheet and pastry into the refrigerator for a few minutes while you make the filling.

Preheat oven to 400°F. Put plums into a bowl.

In a separate bowl, mix sugar and cornstarch, then stir into plums. Stir in lemon juice. Set aside.

Remove pastry from refrigerator. Imagine an 8-inch circle in the center of the rolled-out pastry. Sprinkle cornmeal evenly in that circle. Using a slotted spoon, lift plums out of juice (do not discard juice) and spread evenly over cornmeal. Lift pastry by sliding a spatula or dough scraper under the edge, then fold it up over the plums; you want about 2 inches of pastry overlapping the plums all around. (If pastry starts to break, it is still too cold. Wait a minute or two, then continue.) Work your way around the crostata; the pastry will form pleats. Pour juice from the bowl over the exposed plums. Dust the tops of the plums with a few pinches of nutmeg. Lightly brush pastry with milk and sprinkle with sugar. Bake on the center oven rack for 20 minutes. Reduce heat to 375°F and bake for 30 to 35 minutes more, until plums are bubbly and thickened. Check crostata as it bakes. If juice breaks through the crust, sprinkle 2 or 3 additional teaspoons of cornmeal on the sheet at the breach to contain juice. Thoroughly cool crostata on the baking sheet on a cooling rack. Serve warm or at room temperature.

Makes 6 to 8 servings.

Grilled Blueberry Crumble

If you've never used your grill to bake a dessert, try this recipe and find out
what you've been missing. You get all the yumminess of an oven-baked dessert
with the faintest scent of smoke to give the crumble a spicy flavor.
Plus, no need to heat up your kitchen with a hot oven.

3 pints blueberries (wild blueberries
are best, but any fresh
blueberries will do)

¾ cup all-purpose flour, divided

½ cup sugar

2 tablespoons fresh lemon juice

1 teaspoon grated lemon zest

½ cup coarsely crumbled biscotti
or gingersnaps

½ cup brown sugar

6 tablespoons (¾ stick) cold, unsalted
butter, cut into 1-inch pieces

pinch of salt

1 cup wood chips (preferably apple),
soaked in water for 1 hour,
then drained

vanilla ice cream (optional)

FUN FACTS: There are
three types of blueberries:
highbush, lowbush, and
hybrid half-high. The
most commonly planted
blueberry is the highbush.
Different varieties of blueberry
plants produce significantly
different types of fruit, from
tiny and tart purple-blue wild
and lowbush blueberries to
large, bland berries and many
varieties in between. According
to USDA tests, blueberries have
been shown to contain more
antioxidants than 40 other
common fruit and vegetables.

Lightly mist a 10x8-inch aluminum foil pan with
nonstick cooking spray.

In a nonreactive bowl, combine blueberries, ¼ cup of
flour, sugar, lemon juice, and lemon zest, then gently
toss to mix. Spoon blueberry mixture into prepared pan.

In a food processor, combine biscotti crumbles, brown
sugar, and remaining ½ cup of flour. Process until a
coarse powder forms. Add butter and salt, then pulse
until crumbly. Spoon mixture over blueberries.

Set up the grill for indirect grilling and preheat to
medium-high heat. If using a gas grill, place all of the
wood chips in the smoker box and run the grill on high
until you see smoke, then reduce heat to medium-high.
If using a charcoal grill, preheat it to medium-high, then
toss all of the wood chips or chunks on the coals.

Place pan in the center of the hot grate, away from the
heat, and cover the grill. Cook for 40 minutes, or until
blueberry mixture is bubbling and top is browned. Serve
with vanilla ice cream (if using).

Makes 8 servings.

Late Summer Soup With Stone Fruit

Peaches, apricots, nectarines, plums, and cherries share similar traits and
are classified as stone fruit because of the single pit (stony seed) within their
sweet, fleshy fruit. This soup is a brilliant summer celebration of stone fruit
and a great fruit dessert that does not require baking.

SOUP:

1 cup sugar

1 cup Gewürztraminer wine

½ cup table grapes, white or red

½ cup pitted fresh cherries

3 plums, pitted and halved

1 cinnamon stick

1 sprig mint

zest of 1 orange

FRUIT:

2 plums, pitted and halved

2 peaches, pitted and halved

1 kiwifruit, peeled and diced

1 cup fresh cherries, pitted and halved

½ cup raspberries

vanilla ice cream or fruit sorbet

For soup: In a saucepan, simmer 2 cups of water and the
sugar together until sugar dissolves. Add wine, grapes,
cherries, plums, cinnamon stick, mint, and orange zest
and simmer for 30 minutes, or until tender. Remove
cinnamon stick, divide into two batches, purée in a
blender, then strain.

For fruit: Make a series of ⅛-inch-wide vertical cuts in
plums and peaches, leaving enough skin at the top to
hold each half together. Place each peach or plum half
into a single serving bowl, then spread slices out into a
fan shape.

Spoon soup into bowls, topping each with kiwifruit,
cherries, and raspberries and a scoop of vanilla ice cream.

Makes 8 servings.

FUN FACTS: Cherry trees
do not bear fruit until their
fourth year. Once mature,
a single cherry tree can
produce 30 to 50 quarts
of fruit each year. Dwarf cherry
trees bear fruit in their third year
and can produce 10 to 15 quarts of
fruit each year.

Raspberry Honey Cake With Raspberry Sauce

Try to find a local apiary where you can purchase raw honey for this recipe and your other honey needs. Most supermarket honey is processed and devoid of any nutritional or medicinal value. If you choose to use a Bundt pan for this recipe, bake at a lower temperature and for a longer time. Test for doneness periodically.

CAKE:

2 cups honey

1 cup (2 sticks) unsalted butter, softened

2 teaspoons vanilla extract

6 eggs

2 cups whole wheat flour

1 cup all-purpose flour

½ teaspoon baking soda

½ teaspoon salt

½ cup plain yogurt

½ cup sour cream

1 tablespoon grated lemon zest

2 cups raspberries

¼ cup chopped blanched almonds

SAUCE:

2 cups raspberries

⅓ cup sugar

1 tablespoon cornstarch

For cake: Preheat oven to 350°F. Grease and flour a 10-inch tube pan.

In a bowl, cream honey and butter until light. Add vanilla and eggs, beating well after each addition.

In a separate bowl, combine flours, baking soda, and salt. Sift dry ingredients into creamed mixture alternately with yogurt and sour cream, beating after each addition. Fold in lemon zest, raspberries, and almonds. Pour into prepared pan. Bake for 45 to 55 minutes, or until cake pulls away from the side of the pan. Cool on a rack for 10 minutes before inverting onto a serving plate.

For sauce: In a saucepan, combine raspberries, sugar, and cornstarch with ⅓ cup of water. Bring to a boil and stir until sauce is smooth and thickened. If desired, strain through a sieve or cheesecloth to remove seeds.

Serve cake with raspberry sauce drizzled on individual pieces.

Makes 10 servings.

FUN FACT: One cup of raspberries supplies more than 40 percent of the recommended daily intake of vitamin C and manganese and one-third of the fiber that you require every day. In fact, raspberries provide more fiber than any other fresh fruit.

Peach Cobbler

This old-fashioned dessert is always popular and is best with fresh peaches. It comes together quickly and, besides the fresh peaches, calls only for pantry and refrigerator staples.

¼ cup (½ stick) salted butter, melted

4 cups peeled and sliced fresh peaches

1 cup sugar, divided

¼ teaspoon ground nutmeg

¼ teaspoon ground cinnamon

1 cup all-purpose flour

2 teaspoons baking powder

¾ cup milk

raw sugar, for topping (optional)

whipped cream (optional)

Preheat oven to 400°F.

Pour butter into a 13x9-inch baking pan. Add peaches. Sprinkle ½ cup of sugar over peaches, dust with nutmeg and cinnamon, and stir together.

In a bowl, combine remaining ½ cup of sugar, flour, baking powder, and milk. Stir until smooth. Pour over peaches. Sprinkle with raw sugar (if using). Bake for 30 to 40 minutes, or until top is golden. Serve with whipped cream (if using).

Makes 6 to 8 servings.

Plum Cake With Almond Streusel

You may substitute regular plums in this recipe, but the smaller Italian prune plums are sweeter. This is a great cake to make for breakfast because the dough can rise overnight in the refrigerator.

DOUGH:

⅓ cup lukewarm (105° to 115°F) water, plus more as needed

1 package (2¼ teaspoons) active dry yeast

2 cups all-purpose flour

1 tablespoon sugar

¾ teaspoon salt

½ cup (1 stick) unsalted butter, softened

1 egg

12 to 14 Italian prune plums or 9 regular plums

TOPPING:

½ cup firmly packed brown sugar

⅓ cup all-purpose flour

½ teaspoon salt

2 tablespoons (¼ stick) butter, softened

½ cup blanched almond slices, lightly crushed

FUN FACTS: Most plums fall into one of two categories: European and Japanese. European plums, also known as prune plums, tend to be smaller and sweeter and dry easily. Japanese varieties are larger and juicier but are not as cold-hardy. European plums are self-pollinating, while Japanese plums must be grown with a second Japanese variety in order to set fruit.

For dough: In a bowl, whisk together lukewarm water and yeast; set aside.

In the bowl of a stand mixer or food processor fitted with a dough blade, combine flour, sugar, salt, butter, and egg. Add yeast mixture and pulse until a ball forms. It should be sticky; add more water, a tablespoon at a time, if needed. Remove dough from processor and transfer to a lightly oiled bowl. Cover with plastic wrap and refrigerate overnight. It will rise only slightly.

When dough is ready, adjust oven rack to middle position and preheat to 400°F. Grease a 9-inch springform pan.

Remove dough from refrigerator and set aside. Halve plums (if using regular plums, cut into quarters) and remove pits, then set aside.

For topping: In a bowl, combine brown sugar, flour, salt, and butter. Rub mixture with your fingers until crumbly, then stir in almonds and set aside.

Remove dough from plastic wrap and, on a lightly floured work surface, press with your fingers into a 9-inch circle. Place dough in prepared pan. Leaving a ½-inch border around edge of dough, arrange plums snugly, like fallen dominoes, in circles over surface of dough.

Sprinkle topping on plums. Bake for 40 to 45 minutes, or until topping and crust are light brown.

Makes 8 servings.

Fall Recipes

With its cooling temperatures and abundant harvest of distinct and robust foods, fall is a wonderful time to enjoy the fruit (and vegetables!) of your labor. While apples and pumpkins get much of the glory and hype in this season, there is actually a huge variety of delicious provisions ready for consumption in the fall. Plenty of late-summer vegetables are still available, and cool-weather crops are reaching their peak. Fall flavors come in a complete spectrum of textures and temptations, and the recipes in this chapter offer everything from simple and filling fare to fresh options for holiday feasts. Whether you're planning ahead to preserve some of the garden's yield for later months or have company with whom you want to share a winning dish or dessert, fall provides more than enough options from its nourishing bounty.

Beet Chips

These yummy beet chips are great as a snack—alone or with a dip such as hummus—or use them to crunch up a green salad. Beets come in many shades, including solids of deep red, bright red, pink, yellow, and white, as well as in striped varieties. Any variety of beet works well in this recipe.

4 beets, stems and greens removed, cut into very thin slices

1 tablespoon olive oil

½ teaspoon sea salt

HARVEST TIP:
• Beets can survive frost and almost-freezing temperatures, which makes them a great choice for northern gardeners and an excellent long-season crop.

• Fresh beets can be stored in the refrigerator for 5 to 7 days. Clipping the greens off beets will keep them fresher longer. Leave about 1 inch of stem on each beet and store the greens separately.

Preheat oven to 400°F. Get out a large baking sheet.

Place beets in a bowl, then add olive oil and salt. Toss to combine.

Place beets in a single layer on baking sheet. Do not overlap slices; use multiple baking sheets if needed for space. Bake for 45 minutes to 1 hour, turning slices over about halfway through cooking time. Watch carefully to prevent burning, especially if some chips are thinner than others. Remove from oven when chips are crispy. Cool before eating.

Makes 4 servings.

Green Tomato Salsa

In some years, the first frost arrives early and you're left with a load of unripened (green) tomatoes. Don't let them die on the vine. Instead, use them up in this tempting salsa.

1 red bell pepper, sliced in half and seeded

2 jalapeño peppers, sliced in half and seeded

4 to 5 green tomatoes, chopped

3 cloves garlic, minced

2 onions, chopped

1 teaspoon sugar

1 teaspoon ground cumin

½ cup chopped fresh cilantro or parsley

salt and freshly ground black pepper, to taste

Preheat grill or prepare oven broiler. Get out a baking sheet.

Place peppers on baking sheet and grill or broil, turning until skins blister, blacken, and can be easily peeled. Remove from grill or broiler and set aside until cool enough to handle. Peel and chop peppers.

In a bowl, combine peppers, tomatoes, garlic, onions, sugar, cumin, and cilantro. Season with salt and pepper, then refrigerate for at least 3 hours. Serve with chips or atop your favorite Mexican entrée.

Makes 3 cups.

Cinnamon Applesauce

This is a delicious treat straight from the jar or pair it with grilled pork chops or potato cakes if you prefer to mix your sweet with savory.

8 assorted apples (any varieties), peeled, cored, and cut into chunks

1 tablespoon fresh lemon juice

1 cup apple cider

½ cup sugar

1 cinnamon stick

2 tablespoons apple or pear brandy (optional)

In a saucepan, toss apples with lemon juice. Add cider, sugar, and cinnamon and bring to a boil.

Reduce to a simmer and cook for 15 minutes, or until tender. Let cool for 20 minutes. Discard cinnamon stick.

Mash apples to preferred consistency. Stir in brandy (if using). Cool to room temperature, then cover and refrigerate.

Makes 4 cups.

STORAGE TIPS:
• If you plan to store apples, select late-season fruit that are in perfect condition, with no bruises or blemishes that could provide entry points for rot.

• The ideal storage space is somewhere dark, well-ventilated, and cool but frost-free. Most garages and sheds are ideal, while attics and basements should be avoided due to excessive heat, lack of ventilation, or low humidity.

Southwestern Pumpkin Hummus

You'll need about one pound of puréed pumpkin for this recipe. You can use canned pumpkin purée or follow the instructions on page 99 to make your own purée from fresh pumpkins. Note that this recipe calls for refrigerating the hummus overnight.

scant 2 cups puréed cooked pumpkin or 1 can (15 ounces) pumpkin purée

8 cloves garlic

¼ cup fresh cilantro

¼ cup fresh lime juice

¼ cup tahini paste

2 tablespoons pumpkin oil or olive oil

3 teaspoons ground cumin

1 teaspoon salt

½ teaspoon chili powder

½ teaspoon chipotle pepper (ground or flakes)

pumpkin seeds, for garnish

sesame seeds, for garnish

chopped fresh herbs, for garnish

In a food processor, combine pumpkin, garlic, cilantro, lime juice, tahini, oil, cumin, salt, chili powder, and chipotle pepper. Process until smooth. Transfer to a bowl and cover. Refrigerate overnight.

Before serving, garnish with pumpkin seeds, sesame seeds, and herbs, and drizzle with oil. Serve with vegetables, crackers, or tortilla chips.

Makes 2 to 2½ cups.

COOKING TIP: Be sure to save the seeds when preparing your pumpkin for baking. To roast the seeds, preheat oven to 350°F. Rinse seeds, toss with a little olive oil, and spread on a rimmed baking sheet. Sprinkle with salt and bake for about 15 minutes, stirring seeds about halfway through.

Soy-Glazed Green Beans With Crispy Shallots

This is a savory holiday alternative to the green bean casserole flavored
with cream of mushroom soup and topped with a can of fried onions.
We're not looking to usurp anyone's sacred dish, but think of
this as a fresh-from-the-garden variation on the classic.

½ cup plus 2 tablespoons vegetable
oil, divided

2 large shallots, thinly sliced crosswise

½ teaspoon kosher or sea salt

10 cups green beans, trimmed

5 cloves garlic, thinly sliced

¼ cup soy sauce

2 tablespoons maple syrup

GROWING TIPS:
• Plant shallot sets 3 to 5
inches apart in rows 18 to 24
inches apart. You can also
grow shallots in pots if you
don't have a larger garden space.

• Shallots can be harvested anytime
during the growing season. If they
are harvested early, you can use
young shallots as you would
use scallions.

• Shallots should be cured in a dry,
dark place, and bulbs can be stored
for up to 6 months.

In a skillet over medium-high heat, warm ½ cup of oil
until it shimmers. Add shallots and salt; cook, stirring,
until browned and crispy, 8 to 10 minutes. Strain
shallots from oil and set aside on a paper towel.

Fill a saucepan with 2 inches of water and set a steamer
basket inside. Arrange beans in basket, cover, and bring
water to a boil over high heat. Steam beans for about
6 minutes, or until almost tender; then drain and set
beans aside.

In a large skillet over medium-high heat, warm the
remaining 2 tablespoons of oil. Add garlic and cook for
1 minute; then add beans, 2 tablespoons of water, soy
sauce, and maple syrup. Cook, stirring often, for 6 to 8
minutes, or until beans are tender. Sprinkle with fried
shallots and serve.

Makes 8 servings.

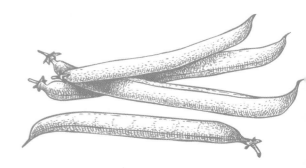

Herb Butter

This herb butter is a marvelous way to preserve your garden-fresh herbs for later enjoyment. Make and freeze this flavorful butter when you have access to lots of fresh herbs, then slice off however much you need to add something special to cooked vegetables, prepared steak, warm bread, and sandwiches.

1 pound (4 sticks) butter, softened

1 clove garlic, minced

1 shallot, minced

½ tube (1.6 ounces) anchovy paste

½ bunch fresh parsley, chopped

2 tablespoons chopped fresh basil

2 tablespoons chopped fresh thyme

2 tablespoons Worcestershire sauce

½ teaspoon paprika

½ teaspoon freshly ground
    black pepper

Using an electric hand or stand mixer, beat butter until fluffy. Add garlic, shallots, anchovy paste, parsley, basil, thyme, Worcestershire, paprika, and pepper and mix until fully incorporated. Remove butter from bowl to a sheet of aluminum foil and form into a log. Wrap foil around butter log, twisting the ends of foil to seal. Freeze, then slice as needed.

Makes one 1-pound log.

 HARVEST TIP: Fresh herbs can transform meals into something really special, but many herbs die back in winter, so it's worth preserving your harvest before this happens to ensure a continued supply through to the following spring. Air-drying, microwave drying, freezing, and mixing into butter, vinegars, or oils are all excellent preserving methods that are easy to do with both small and large quantities of herbs.

Pumpkin Biscuits

You can substitute another variety of squash for the pumpkin if you prefer.

½ cup milk

½ cup puréed cooked pumpkin

¼ cup (½ stick) butter

¼ cup sugar

2 teaspoons pumpkin pie spice

½ teaspoon salt

1 packet (2¼ teaspoons) yeast dissolved in ¼ cup lukewarm (105° to 115°F) water

2½ cups all-purpose flour

 COOKING TIP: To make pumpkin purée, preheat oven to 325°F. Scrub the outside of the pumpkin with a vegetable brush to remove any dirt. Cut the pumpkin in half and use a spoon to scrape out the fibers and the seeds. A serrated grapefruit spoon works great for this. (Save seeds for roasting separately; see cooking tip on page 94.) Cut the pumpkin halves into smaller pieces, then place them skin side up in a shallow baking dish. Add just enough water to cover the bottom of the dish and cover tightly with aluminum foil. Bake until the pumpkin is fork-tender. The baking time will vary depending on the size of pumpkin pieces. Let pumpkin cool, and then either cut off the peel or scoop out the flesh. Purée pumpkin flesh in a food processor until smooth.

In a saucepan, scald milk and then immediately remove it from heat. Add pumpkin, butter, sugar, pumpkin pie spice, and salt to milk and stir to combine. Cool to lukewarm, then add dissolved yeast and flour; cover and put in a warm place to let double in bulk, about 2 hours.

Preheat oven to 375°F. Grease a baking sheet.

Cut dough into 12 equal biscuits. Place biscuits side by side on prepared baking sheet and let rise again for 30 minutes. Bake for 12 to 15 minutes.

Makes 12 biscuits.

Parsnip and Carrot Tart

Both parsnips and carrots are especially tasty if harvested after a couple of frosts, so think of this savory tart as the perfect meal to welcome in the season of cold but cozy weather.

CRUST:

1 cup all-purpose flour

3 tablespoons sugar

5 tablespoons butter, cut into pieces

1 egg yolk

FILLING:

2 cups shredded peeled carrots

2 cups shredded peeled parsnips

⅔ cup sugar

2 tablespoons all-purpose flour

1½ teaspoons grated orange zest

1½ teaspoons grated lemon zest

1 cup lemon-flavor yogurt

3 eggs

½ cup pecan halves

For crust: Adjust oven rack to center position and preheat oven to 325°F. Get out a 9-inch tart pan with removable bottom.

In a food processor, combine flour and sugar. Add butter, a few pieces at a time, and process until fine crumbs form. Add egg yolk and process until dough holds together when pressed. Press dough over the bottom and up the sides of the tart pan. Bake for 15 minutes, or until crust is very lightly browned. Remove from oven and set aside. Do not turn off oven.

For filling: In a skillet over high heat, add carrots, parsnips, and ¾ cup of water. Bring to a boil, cover, and reduce heat to low. Simmer for about 6 minutes, stirring occasionally, until the vegetables are soft and the liquid has evaporated. Remove from heat and set aside to cool.

In a bowl, combine sugar, flour, orange zest, lemon zest, yogurt, and eggs and whisk until blended. Stir in vegetable mixture until fully combined. Pour into prepared crust. Arrange pecans on top in a decorative pattern.

Bake for 35 to 40 minutes, or until center does not jiggle when pan is tapped. Move tart to a wire rack to cool completely. Once cool, cover and chill in the refrigerator.

To serve, run a knife between the crust and side of pan to loosen, then remove the sides of pan.

Makes 8 servings.

Roasted Beets and Chèvre Over Beet Greens Couscous

Roasted beets and creamy chèvre are a wonderful flavor and texture pairing in this robust salad. Enjoy it with your favorite herbed chèvre or use this recipe as a reason to seek out a local dairy or cheese maker at your farmers' market.

10 small beets, multicolor if available, with 4 cups greens

¾ cup raspberry walnut vinaigrette bottled dressing, divided

½ teaspoon freshly ground black pepper, divided

⅓ cup roughly chopped walnuts

3 tablespoons walnut oil or olive oil, divided

¾ cup thinly sliced shallots or mild onion

4 cups cooked couscous

½ teaspoon kosher salt

½ cup herbed chèvre, crumbled

2 tablespoons chopped fresh tarragon (optional)

Remove greens from beet roots. Wash and peel beets. Wash, then roughly chop greens; set aside. Slice beets lengthwise. In a shallow ovenproof dish, toss beets with ½ cup of dressing. Allow to marinate for at least 30 minutes; if longer—up to overnight—refrigerate.

Adjust oven rack to center position and preheat oven to 350°F. Get out a baking sheet.

Drain beets, discarding marinade, then season with ¼ teaspoon of pepper. Put beets on baking sheet and roast for 45 minutes, or until tender.

In a nonstick skillet over medium heat, toast nuts for about 5 minutes, shaking the pan to prevent burning. Remove nuts from pan and set aside to cool.

Return skillet to the heat, warm 2 tablespoons of oil, then add shallots and cook until they begin to caramelize. Add beet greens and cook for another 3 minutes, or until tender. Add couscous, remaining 1 tablespoon of oil, salt, and remaining ¼ teaspoon of pepper. Stir to blend and heat through. Remove from heat.

Serve couscous mixture topped with roasted beets, crumbled cheese, and nuts. Drizzle with remaining dressing and scatter tarragon (if using) on top.

Makes 4 servings.

Kale Salad With Cranberries, Feta, and Walnuts

When preparing this salad, it's important to remove the ribs from the kale leaves and then slice the kale into thin strips as instructed. If this still seems like too much kale for your taste, you can combine kale and spinach in this salad and still have a hearty, tasty dish.

1 big bunch green-leaf kale (to make about 8 cups of thinly sliced leaves)

1½ tablespoons rice-wine vinegar, red-wine vinegar, or apple cider vinegar

1½ teaspoons minced shallots

kosher or sea salt, to taste

6 tablespoons extra-virgin olive oil

freshly ground black pepper, to taste

⅓ cup roughly chopped dried cranberries

⅓ cup roughly chopped toasted walnuts

⅓ cup crumbled feta cheese

1 tablespoon fresh lemon or lime juice

Remove stems from kale and discard. Wash and spin kale leaves in a salad spinner or blot between paper towels until thoroughly dry. Slice kale thinly (¼- to ½-inch wide), place in a bowl, and set aside.

In a separate bowl, whisk together vinegar, shallots, and a pinch of salt. Let stand for about 10 minutes. Slowly whisk in olive oil, adding pepper and more salt, if desired. Pour dressing over kale and toss well. Mix in cranberries, walnuts, feta, and lemon juice. Serve immediately or refrigerate for up to 3 days.

Makes about 6 servings.

HARVEST TIPS:
• Kale will continue growing until the temperature dips below 20°F. It tastes even sweeter after a touch of frost.

• Kale is ready to harvest when the leaves are about the size of your hand.

• Pick about one fistful of leaves per harvest. Avoid picking the terminal bud (found at the top center of the plant) because this will help to keep the plant productive.

Acorn Squash Succotash

This recipe is simple and delicious, a perfect holiday standard. These flavors work well with all kinds of winter squash, so try this dish with your favorite variety or whatever kind grew in abundance in your garden this year.

2 tablespoons olive oil

1 onion, chopped

1 clove garlic, minced

1 red bell pepper, chopped

1 acorn squash, peeled, seeded, and cut into ½-inch cubes

1½ cups chicken broth

1 cup fresh or frozen corn

1 cup fresh or frozen peas

¾ cup heavy cream

1¼ teaspoons chopped fresh thyme

salt and freshly ground black pepper, to taste

In a skillet over medium heat, warm oil. Add onions and garlic and cook, stirring frequently, for about 5 minutes, or until they begin to turn brown. Add peppers and cook for 3 to 5 minutes. Add squash and chicken broth. Bring to a boil, then lower heat and simmer for about 10 minutes, or until squash is almost tender, but not soft. Add corn, peas, cream, and thyme. Simmer for 5 minutes, season with salt and pepper, and serve.

Makes 6 to 8 servings.

Maple-Butternut Squash Casserole

Maple syrup and winter squash make a palate-pleasing combination. The flavor of the combined spices used in this recipe is very close to that of pumpkin pie spice, so feel free to substitute 1¼ to 1½ teaspoons of pumpkin pie spice if that's what you have in your spice collection.

1 large or 2 small butternut squashes, cut into ½-inch cubes

1 cup dried fruit (such as cranberries, blueberries, chopped apricots)

½ cup (1 stick) butter, melted

1 cup maple syrup

½ teaspoon ground nutmeg

¼ teaspoon ground cinnamon

¼ teaspoon ground ginger

¼ teaspoon ground cloves

raw almonds, sliced

Adjust oven rack to center position and preheat oven to 350°F. Butter a 13x9-inch baking dish.

In a bowl, combine squash and dried fruit.

In a separate bowl, combine butter, maple syrup, nutmeg, cinnamon, ginger, and cloves. Pour over squash and dried fruit and stir to combine. Pour into prepared dish and bake for 45 minutes, or until squash is tender.

Sprinkle almonds on top of squash and put under broiler for 5 minutes, or until almonds start to brown.

Makes about 10 servings.

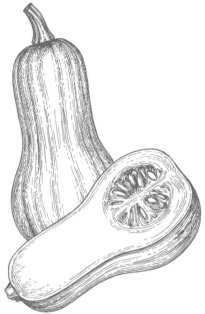

Turkey-Stuffed Eggplant

Looking for a creative way to use leftover turkey? This recipe offers an inspired combination of flavors and textures that will turn leftover turkey into an exciting new meal. If the skin on the eggplant is not to your liking, the stuffing in this recipe can also be used to fill tomatoes or bell peppers.

2 medium eggplants

6 tablespoons (¾ stick) butter

1 pound mushrooms, diced

2 onions, diced

2 cups diced leftover cooked turkey

¼ cup dry white wine

salt and freshly ground black pepper,
    to taste

¼ cup shredded cheese
    (use your favorite)

chopped fresh oregano, for garnish

 FUN FACTS: Eggplants are warm-weather perennials but are typically grown as annuals. Also known as aubergines, eggplants can be grown in a traditional row garden or in containers. Like tomatoes and peppers, eggplants are in the nightshade family of vegetables.

Preheat oven to 400°F. Grease a baking sheet or line with parchment paper.

Cut eggplants in half lengthwise and carefully scoop out pulp, leaving four nice eggplant shells. Dice pulp and set aside.

In a skillet over medium heat, melt butter. Add diced eggplant pulp, mushrooms, and onions and cook for 15 minutes, or until vegetables are soft. Add turkey and stir to combine. Add wine and season with salt and pepper.

Spoon mixture into eggplant shells, mounding it above the shell rims as needed. Place shells on prepared baking sheet. Sprinkle with cheese and bake for 15 minutes. Garnish with oregano before serving.

Makes 4 servings.

Kale Harvest Pie

Kale tastes best after a light frost, making this a good late-season harvest dish. Include a mixture of other greens (Swiss chard, spinach, turnip greens) for varied flavor.

3 pounds untrimmed kale or other greens

3 tablespoons butter, divided

1 tablespoon olive oil

1 onion, finely chopped

2 cloves garlic, minced

1 red or yellow bell pepper, finely chopped

1 small zucchini, shredded

1 carrot, shredded

⅔ cup chopped fresh basil

salt and freshly ground black pepper, to taste

3 eggs, beaten

½ cup grated Parmesan cheese

1 cup fresh bread crumbs

Preheat oven to 375°F. Butter a shallow baking dish or pie plate.

Trim stems and ribs from kale. Chop kale leaves into bite-size pieces.

In a skillet, melt 1 tablespoon butter with olive oil. Add onions and garlic and cook for 2 minutes, stirring constantly. Add kale, peppers, zucchini, carrots, and basil and cook, covered, over medium heat for 10 minutes. Uncover and simmer gently until liquid has evaporated. Season with salt and pepper, then remove skillet from heat and cool slightly.

Add eggs to vegetable mix and stir to combine. Pour vegetables into prepared baking dish. Sprinkle with Parmesan.

In a separate skillet over medium heat, melt remaining 2 tablespoons butter, add bread crumbs, and cook until golden. Sprinkle bread crumbs over pie and bake for 25 minutes. Remove from oven and let cool for 10 minutes before serving.

Makes 6 servings.

Curried Cauliflower, Potatoes, and Peas

Many small farms now grow cauliflower in a variety of colors, from the most common white heads to bright green, soft orange, and bright purple ones. Look for them in your local market and experiment with your favorite.

¼ cup olive oil

2 onions, finely chopped

1 head cauliflower, chopped

1 pound potatoes, peeled and diced

2 tomatoes, chopped

1 teaspoon salt

1 teaspoon ground cumin

½ teaspoon ground turmeric

¼ teaspoon chili powder

1 cup peas or 2 cups cooked chickpeas or 1 pound chopped fresh spinach

½ teaspoon garam masala

In a skillet over medium-high heat, warm oil. Add onions and cook until soft and golden. Stir in cauliflower and potatoes. Add tomatoes, salt, cumin, turmeric, and chili powder; stir and cook for 3 to 4 minutes. Reduce heat to medium-low, cover, and cook for about 15 minutes, or until potatoes and cauliflower are almost tender, stirring from time to time to keep vegetables from sticking. Add peas and cook, covered, for an additional 5 to 7 minutes. Sprinkle with garam masala and stir gently to mix. Serve hot.

Makes 4 to 6 servings.

Squash Risotto

Make this recipe with leftover acorn or butternut squash (mashed sweet potatoes work well, too). One of the keys to successful risotto is to keep the stock hot so that when you add it to the rice, it doesn't cool everything down.

4 cups turkey or chicken stock

2 tablespoons unsalted butter

1 onion, finely diced

3 cups Arborio or Carnaroli rice

2 cups mashed cooked squash

½ cup grated Parmesan cheese

COOKING TIP: To make your own turkey stock, combine 1 turkey carcass (plus leftover bits of meat), 2½ quarts cold water, 4 carrots (peeled and chopped), 2 cloves garlic (chopped), 2 teaspoons dried thyme or sage, ¼ cup celery leaves, 1 bay leaf, and salt and pepper, to taste, in a stockpot. Simmer for 2 hours, partially covered. Skim occasionally. Strain through cheesecloth. Cool, chill, and skim fat from top.

In a saucepan over high heat, bring turkey stock to a boil. Reduce heat to low and maintain at a simmer.

In a separate saucepan over medium-high heat, melt butter and sauté onions for 5 minutes, or until translucent. Add rice and stir well to coat. Cook, stirring often, for 3 minutes, being careful not to brown rice or onion.

Add 1½ cups hot stock to rice mixture and stir continuously until most of the liquid is absorbed. Add another 1 cup hot stock and stir until most of the liquid is absorbed. Repeat with another 1 cup hot stock until rice is barely al dente.

Add squash and remaining stock. Cook for 1 minute. Add Parmesan and stir until well incorporated.

Makes 6 servings.

Autumn Garden Soup

If you can't find fresh shell beans for this recipe, you can substitute ½ cup dried
navy beans or soldier beans cooked in unsalted water or fresh green or wax beans.
For details on how to prepare pumpkin purée, see the cooking tip on page 99.

1 ham bone

¼ cup chopped salt pork

3 stalks celery, chopped,
    or handful of celery leaves

2 onions, chopped

2 carrots, peeled and diced

1 clove garlic, chopped

several sprigs parsley

1 cup fresh shell beans
    (see recipe note)

a few leaves each of fresh mint,
    marjoram, basil, rosemary,
    and thyme

4 tomatoes, peeled and diced

½ pound fresh spinach or other
    greens, trimmed and chopped

1 cup puréed cooked winter squash
    or pumpkin

salt and freshly ground black pepper,
    to taste

grated cheese, for garnish

In a pot over medium heat, cover ham bone with water
and simmer for 1 hour.

In a skillet over medium heat, cook salt pork until fat is
released. Add celery, onions, carrots, garlic, and parsley
and cook lightly, without browning. Set aside until broth
is ready.

Remove ham bone from pot and skim any fat from
the stock. Cut off any bits of meat from ham bone and
return them to the soup. Add vegetable mixture to broth
and simmer for 1 hour.

Add beans, herbs, tomatoes, spinach, and squash to
soup and simmer for 30 minutes. Season with salt and
pepper. Serve hot with a sprinkling of grated cheese.

Makes 4 to 6 servings.

Carrot Ginger Soup

This soup comes together quickly and, because of its yummy
yet mild flavor, tends to be a family favorite.

2 tablespoons (¼ stick) butter

2 leeks, chopped

1 pound carrots, peeled and diced

1 pound potatoes, peeled and diced

zest and juice of 1 orange

1 teaspoon chopped fresh ginger

1 teaspoon brown sugar

4 cups vegetable broth

1 cup milk

salt, to taste

splash of dry sherry, to taste

dash of ground nutmeg, to taste

chopped fresh parsley or cilantro,
    for garnish

COOKING TIP: Not sure
what to do with leftover
ginger? Steep a few slices
of the fresh root in a cup
of hot water for a lovely
ginger tea. Add a touch of lemon
and/or honey to make the flavor a
bit gentler.

In a pot over medium heat, melt butter. Add leeks and
cook until soft. Add carrots, potatoes, orange zest and
juice, ginger, and brown sugar. Cook for 5 to 7 minutes,
or until vegetables have softened. Add broth and milk
and bring to a low boil. As soon as soup starts to boil,
turn down heat and simmer for 20 minutes.

Cool slightly, then transfer soup to a blender or food
processor and purée in batches. Return to pot and heat
to desired serving temperature. Season with salt, sherry,
and nutmeg. Garnish with parsley and serve.

Makes 4 to 6 servings.

Roasted Autumn Vegetables

Hearty root vegetables taste phenomenal when roasted, and this recipe provides a simple way to do it. All that you really need is olive oil, seasoning, and a few quick steps. This makes a wonderful side dish or a complete meal when served over quinoa or rice.

1 pound small red-skinned potatoes, quartered, or whole creamer potatoes

2 cups peeled, diced butternut squash, cut into ½-inch cubes

2 carrots, peeled and cut into ½-inch-thick diagonal slices

2 parsnips, peeled and cut into ½-inch-thick diagonal slices

2 to 3 cups chopped kale

3 tablespoons olive oil

1 tablespoon chopped fresh rosemary or 1 teaspoon dried rosemary

2 cloves garlic, minced

salt and freshly ground black pepper, to taste

Preheat oven to 450°F. Lightly oil two large, rimmed baking sheets.

In a bowl, combine potatoes, squash, carrots, parsnips, kale, oil, rosemary, garlic, salt, and pepper and toss to coat all evenly. Spread vegetables onto the baking sheets and bake for 15 minutes on separate oven racks. After 15 minutes, stir vegetables and return to oven, switching the placement of the baking sheets. Bake for 15 minutes more, or until the vegetables are tender and browned.

Makes 6 servings.

Not-Too-Spicy Veggie and Lentil Chili

This one-pot soup recipe combines a tasty variety of vegetables with the nutritional punch of legumes. It requires a pressure cooker or slow cooker.

½ pound dried red or green lentils

4 to 5 carrots, diced

4 to 6 cloves garlic, minced

1 to 2 bell peppers, diced

1 red onion, chopped

1 cup diced tomatoes

1 cup fresh or frozen corn kernels

1 cup fresh or frozen shelled
    edamame

1 cup fresh or frozen chopped spinach

2 tablespoons apple cider vinegar

2 tablespoons smoked paprika

2 tablespoons dried parsley

2 teaspoons dried oregano

1 to 2 teaspoons cayenne pepper or
    1 tablespoon hot sauce,
    or to taste

1 teaspoon dried thyme

1 teaspoon dried basil

1 teaspoon curry powder

1 bouillon cube

salt and freshly ground black pepper,
    to taste

tahini, guacamole, and oyster crackers
    (optional toppings)

sour cream or shredded cheese
    (optional toppings)

In an electric pressure cooker or slow cooker, combine lentils, carrots, garlic, bell peppers, onions, tomatoes, corn, edamame, spinach, vinegar, paprika, parsley, oregano, cayenne, thyme, basil, curry powder, bouillon cube, and salt and pepper. Add enough water to cover.

For electric pressure cooker: Set cooker for 11 minutes and start. When time has completed, let sit for 10 minutes before releasing the pressure valve.

For slow cooker: Cook on high for 2 to 3 hours or low for 6 to 8 hours.

Serve over rice or pasta or with baked potatoes or cornbread as a side. Top with tahini, guacamole, oyster crackers, sour cream, or cheese (if using).

Makes 6 servings.

Chicken, Apple, and Cheese Casserole

The combination of apples and Swiss cheese in this dish is lovely, and preparation is easy. Use Jonagold apples or any other variety firm enough to hold up when cooked.

5 tablespoons butter, softened, divided

3 medium-firm apples, halved, cored, and sliced

2 onions, thinly sliced

6 boneless, skinless chicken breast halves

1 teaspoon salt

¼ teaspoon freshly ground black pepper

½ cup shredded Swiss cheese

½ cup grated Parmesan cheese

¼ cup dry bread crumbs

½ teaspoon dried thyme

2 tablespoons brandy or apple cider

Preheat oven to 350°F. Use 1 tablespoon of butter to grease a 2-quart baking dish.

In a heavy skillet over medium heat, melt remaining 4 tablespoons of butter. Add apples and onions and cook until apples are tender, about 10 minutes. Spoon apple mixture into prepared baking dish.

Rub chicken with salt and pepper and arrange breasts over apple–onion mixture.

In a bowl, combine cheeses and bread crumbs, then mix in thyme. Sprinkle cheese–crumb mixture over chicken. Drizzle brandy over all and bake for 35 minutes, or until cheese is golden brown and chicken reaches 165°F on an instant-read thermometer.

Makes 6 servings.

Southwestern Pumpkin Burgers

Here's a meatless burger that even meat eaters will love. You can serve these on toasted buns with standard burger fixings or with no add-ons other than some ranch dressing as a dipping sauce.

3 tablespoons vegetable oil, divided

½ cup finely chopped onion

½ cup fresh or frozen (and thawed) corn kernels

¼ cup finely chopped green bell pepper

1 clove garlic, minced

1 teaspoon ground cumin

1 teaspoon chili powder

½ teaspoon smoked paprika

¾ cup fine-curd cottage cheese

½ cup puréed cooked pumpkin (recipe on page 99)

1 egg yolk

2 tablespoons chopped fresh Italian parsley

scant ½ teaspoon salt

freshly ground black pepper, to taste

1¼ cups panko bread crumbs

1 cup shredded pepper jack or sharp cheddar cheese

In a skillet over medium heat, warm 2 tablespoons of oil. Add onions, corn, and bell peppers and cook for 5 minutes, or until soft. Add garlic, cumin, chili powder, and paprika and cook for 30 seconds more, stirring constantly. Remove from heat.

In a bowl, combine cottage cheese, pumpkin, and egg yolk and mix with a wooden spoon. Add onion–corn–pepper mixture, parsley, salt, and black pepper and stir to combine. Add bread crumbs and cheese and stir to combine. Cover bowl and refrigerate for at least 2 hours, or overnight.

In a nonstick skillet over medium heat, warm remaining 1 tablespoon of oil. Shape chilled pumpkin mixture into six ¾-inch-thick patties. Place them in the skillet and cook, in batches if necessary for space, for 3 minutes on each side, or until lightly browned, turning once. Serve warm.

Makes 6 servings.

Roasted Chicken With Root Vegetables

Filled with the robust flavors of turnips, beets, rosemary, and more,
this warming meal is just the ticket for a chilly fall evening.

1 chicken (3 pounds)

2 tablespoons canola oil, divided

kosher or sea salt, to taste

2 sprigs fresh rosemary

1 orange, quartered

1 turnip, peeled and cut into 1-inch
pieces

4 to 6 red or yellow beets, peeled and
halved if small, quartered if large

2 yellow onions, quartered

3 carrots, peeled

freshly ground black pepper, to taste

FUN FACTS:
• Turnips can be grown as
a spring or fall crop (avoid
the heat of summer), but a
fall crop is usually preferred
because it is sweeter and more
tender than the spring crop and
less susceptible to pests than in
springtime.

• Turnips germinate in only a few
days. Within a month, you can
enjoy their bright greens, and
within a second month, you can
eat the swollen roots.

• Turnips make a good substitute
for potatoes.

Preheat oven to 450°F. Get out a roasting dish.

Rub surface of chicken with 1 tablespoon of oil and
season with a few pinches of salt. Place rosemary in
cavity. Lightly squeeze orange pieces to release juices
and place in cavity.

Scatter turnips, beets, onions, and carrots in roasting
dish. Toss with remaining 1 tablespoon of oil and
season with salt and pepper. Place chicken, breast side
up, on top of vegetables. Roast for 30 minutes, then
lower oven to 350°F and roast for 30 to 45 minutes
longer, or until a thermometer inserted into a thigh
reads 165°F.

Remove from oven and let rest for 20 minutes before
slicing. Serve sliced chicken with roasted vegetables
and pan juices.

Makes 4 servings.

Pork With Apples

Pork and apples are a classic combination that perfectly mixes sweet with savory. This dish can also be made in a slow cooker; simply follow the directions for cooking pork.

3 to 4 pounds lean pork, cut into large chunks

6 cups applesauce

2 tablespoons apple pie spice

6 small red-skinned potatoes

4 carrots, peeled and coarsely chopped

2 cups white pearl onions

salt and freshly ground black pepper, to taste

2 firm tart apples, peeled, cored, and thinly sliced

 FUN FACTS: Packaged apple pie spice and pumpkin pie spice are sometimes the same mix of ground spices. (The exact mix depends on the manufacturer.) However, even if the spices are the same, the balance of spices is likely to be different. It's all about the ratio of cinnamon with some variation of ginger, nutmeg, cloves, allspice, and cardamom

In a pot over medium heat, combine pork, applesauce, and apple pie spice. Cover and cook for 10 minutes. Reduce heat and simmer for 4 hours.

At 1 to 1½ hours into cooking time, add potatoes, carrots, and onions to pork mixture and stir to combine. Season with salt and pepper.

At 3 hours and 45 minutes into cooking time, add apple slices and stir to combine.

When 4 hours have elapsed, use a slotted spoon to remove pork, vegetables, and apples from the pot to a serving dish. Pour 1 cup of the sauce over all and serve remaining sauce on the side.

Makes 6 to 8 servings.

Roasted Garlic and Sweet Potato Mac-'n'-Cheese

Looking to elevate mac-'n'-cheese to something special? This recipe accomplishes that by adding an abundance of flavor and some excellent nutrients. We think that you'll love this variation on the classic!

10 whole cloves garlic, peeled, plus 3 cloves, minced

4 tablespoons extra-virgin olive oil, divided

1 pound sweet potatoes, peeled and sliced ¼-inch thick

12 ounces macaroni elbows

4 tablespoons (½ stick) butter

4 tablespoons all-purpose flour

½ teaspoon salt

⅛ teaspoon freshly ground black pepper

3 cups half-and-half

2 cups shredded Italian blend cheese, divided

¾ cup grated Asiago cheese, divided

pinch of dried rosemary

¼ cup panko bread crumbs

Preheat oven to 350°F. Butter a 2-quart baking dish.

Place whole, peeled garlic on a sheet of aluminum foil, drizzle with 2 tablespoons of olive oil, and wrap tightly. Roast for 20 minutes, or until golden. Remove garlic from foil, mash, and set aside.

Fill a pot with water and place over high heat. Add sweet potato slices and bring to a boil. Cook for 6 minutes, or until sweet potato is fork-tender. Drain and set sweet potatoes aside.

In a skillet over medium heat, warm 1 tablespoon of olive oil. Add sweet potato slices and cook until caramelized. Remove from skillet and dice into cubes; set aside.

Bring a pot of water to a boil and add macaroni. Cook for 8 minutes, stirring often. Drain, then set pasta aside.

In the same pot, melt butter over low heat. Add flour, stirring constantly for 3 minutes. Add salt and pepper and whisk in half-and-half. Increase heat to medium and bring sauce to a boil. Turn off heat and add 1¾ cups Italian blend cheese and ½ cup Asiago. Whisk until smooth, then add mashed roasted garlic, sweet potatoes, rosemary, minced garlic, and pasta. Stir to combine, then pour into prepared baking dish.

In a bowl, combine bread crumbs with remaining ¼ cup Italian blend cheese, ¼ cup Asiago, and 1 tablespoon olive oil. Sprinkle bread crumb–cheese mixture over macaroni mixture and bake for 25 to 30 minutes, or until bubbling and golden brown.

Makes 6 servings.

Chicken Fajita-Topped Potatoes

This recipe takes baked potato toppings to a whole new level with delicious chicken fajita fixin's piled onto a steaming fluffy potato.

4 potatoes, scrubbed

1 jalapeño pepper, seeded and chopped

½ cup chicken broth

3 tablespoons oil, divided

1 red bell pepper, chopped

1 sweet onion, sliced vertically

4 boneless, skinless chicken breast halves, thinly sliced

chopped scallions, for garnish

chopped fresh cilantro, for garnish

salsa, for topping

HARVEST TIPS:
• Whether you dig your own potatoes or buy them at a market, don't wash them until right before you use them. Washing potatoes shortens their storage life.

• Allow freshly dug potatoes to sit in a dry, cool place (45° to 60°F) for up to 2 weeks. This allows their skins to "cure," which will help them to keep longer.

• After curing, make sure that you brush off any soil clinging to the potatoes, then store them in a cool, dry, dark place. The ideal temperature for storage is 35° to 40°F.

• Do not store potatoes with apples; the ethylene gas in apples will cause potatoes to spoil.

Preheat oven to 425°F.

Poke holes into the potatoes using a fork, then place on a baking sheet. Bake for 45 to 55 minutes, or until tender.

In a blender or food processor, purée jalapeño and broth and set aside.

In a skillet over medium heat, warm 1 tablespoon of oil. Add bell peppers and cook for 1 minute, stirring constantly. Remove peppers with a slotted spoon and set aside. Add 1 tablespoon of oil to skillet and cook onions for 30 seconds, stirring constantly. Remove onions and set aside with bell peppers. Add remaining 1 tablespoon of oil to skillet, then add chicken and stir-fry for about 2 minutes. Add jalapeño purée to skillet with chicken and cook for 2 minutes more. Return bell peppers and onions to skillet and cook for 1 minute more, or until chicken is cooked through.

Place baked potatoes on a serving plate, slash the tops, and squeeze open. Spoon fajita mixture onto potatoes, garnish with scallions and cilantro, and serve with salsa on the side.

Makes 4 servings.

Potato and Onion Pizza

Potatoes, sweet onions, two cheeses, and rosemary—a scrumptious flavor combination made refreshingly new on a pizza.

Pizza Dough (recipe on page 186)

salt, to taste

7 medium red-skinned potatoes,
    peeled and sliced ⅛-inch thick

3 tablespoons unsalted butter

2 sweet onions, halved and thinly sliced

6 cloves garlic, thinly sliced

cornmeal, for dusting

freshly ground black pepper, to taste

½ cup grated Parmesan cheese

1 tablespoon chopped fresh rosemary

½ cup heavy cream

2 to 3 cups shredded fontina cheese

Follow directions on page 186 to prepare dough.

Lightly oil a large casserole.

Fill a saucepan with lightly salted water and add potatoes. Cover pan with a lid, bring water to a boil, then reduce heat and simmer for 4 minutes, or until potatoes are almost cooked through but still firm, stirring occasionally. Drain, then spread potato slices in prepared casserole to cool.

In a skillet over medium heat, melt butter. Add onions and cook, stirring often, for 7 to 8 minutes, or until soft. Add garlic and cook for 3 to 4 minutes, or until the onions start to turn golden. Set aside.

Lightly flour a clean, dry work surface. When Pizza Dough has doubled, punch it down and turn it out onto the work surface. Divide dough in half and knead into two balls. Let rest for 5 minutes.

Preheat oven to 425°F. Lightly dust two baking sheets with cornmeal.

Working with one ball of dough at a time, roll it into a thin, 12½- to 13-inch circle. Transfer to prepared baking sheet. Pinch around edge of dough so that it's slightly higher than center. Layer on half of the onions, then half of the potatoes, overlapping the potatoes slightly. Season with salt and pepper. Sprinkle with half of Parmesan and half of rosemary. Drizzle with half of cream. Repeat steps with remaining ingredients for the second pizza.

If your oven is large enough, bake pizzas together, on separate oven racks, for 10 to 12 minutes. Remove pizzas from oven and sprinkle evenly with fontina. Return to oven, switching pizzas to opposite racks, and continue baking for another 10 to 12 minutes, or until crust is golden brown around the edges. Transfer pizzas to cooling racks briefly before serving.

Makes 2 pizzas or 6 or more servings.

Browned Butter-Frosted Pumpkin Bars

If you love the taste of pumpkin but pies are not your thing,
try these luscious, pumpkin-spiced bars.

BARS:

1½ cups all-purpose flour

1¼ cups sugar

2 teaspoons baking powder

2 teaspoons ground cinnamon

1 teaspoon baking soda

½ teaspoon ground ginger

scant 2 cups puréed cooked pumpkin
(recipe on page 99)

¾ cup (1½ sticks) salted butter,
melted

3 eggs

¾ cup chopped sweetened dried
cranberries (optional)

FROSTING:

½ cup (1 stick) salted butter

4 cups confectioners' sugar

1 teaspoon vanilla extract

¼ to ⅓ cup milk

Preheat oven to 350°F. Get out a 15x10x1-inch jelly-roll pan.

For bars: In a bowl, combine flour, sugar, baking powder, cinnamon, baking soda, and ginger. Stir in pumpkin, butter, and eggs; mix well. Stir in cranberries (if using). Spread batter into jelly-roll pan. Bake for 20 to 25 minutes, or until a toothpick inserted into the center comes out clean. Cool completely.

For frosting: In a saucepan over medium heat, melt butter, stirring constantly and watching closely, until butter just starts to turn golden brown, about 3 to 5 minutes. Immediately remove from heat, pour into a bowl, and cool for 5 minutes.

Add confectioners' sugar and vanilla to cooled browned butter and mix well. Stir in milk in very small amounts, adding just enough to reach desired frosting consistency. Spread frosting over cooled bars and slice into desired size.

Makes about 5 dozen small bars.

Pumpkin Cookies

Need a pumpkin-flavor treat for on the go? These pillowy soft cookies
are perfect, portable, autumn-scented treats that will satisfy your
pumpkin craving anytime, anywhere.

½ cup (1 stick) butter, softened

1¼ cups brown sugar

2 eggs, beaten

1½ cups puréed cooked pumpkin
(recipe on page 99)

1½ cups all-purpose flour

1 tablespoon baking powder

1 teaspoon ground cinnamon

½ teaspoon ground nutmeg

¼ teaspoon ground ginger

½ teaspoon salt

1 cup chopped walnuts

Preheat oven to 400°F. Get out a baking sheet.

Using an electric hand or stand mixer, cream together
butter and brown sugar. Mix in eggs and pumpkin until
fully incorporated.

In a sifter, combine flour, baking powder, cinnamon,
nutmeg, ginger, and salt, then sift into pumpkin
mixture. Stir to combine, then add nuts. Drop batter
by spoonfuls onto baking sheet. Bake for 15 minutes,
or until lightly browned. Cool slightly on baking sheet,
then move to a cooling rack to cool completely.

Makes about 5 dozen cookies.

Pumpkin Ice Cream Pie

This is for all of the nonbakers who still want to make an amazing pumpkin dessert. This pie requires hardly any actual baking, but has all of the flavor of traditional pie.

CRUST:

1½ cups ground gingersnaps

4½ tablespoons salted butter, melted

FILLING:

3 pints vanilla ice cream

2½ cups puréed cooked pumpkin
(recipe on page 99)

1 teaspoon vanilla extract

1½ teaspoons ground ginger

1½ teaspoons ground cinnamon

½ teaspoon ground allspice

¼ teaspoon salt

TOPPING:

1 cup sour cream

1½ tablespoons maple syrup

pecan halves, for garnish

For crust: Preheat oven to 350°F. Get out a 9-inch deep-dish pie plate.

In a bowl, combine gingersnap crumbs and butter. Press crumbs firmly into pie plate all the way up the sides. Bake for 10 to 15 minutes, or until edges are golden brown. Set aside to cool.

For filling: Remove ice cream from freezer and let sit at room temperature for 15 minutes.

Meanwhile, in a saucepan over medium heat, combine pumpkin, vanilla, ginger, cinnamon, allspice, and salt. Cook for 8 minutes, stirring often.

Using an electric hand or stand mixer, combine ice cream and hot pumpkin mixture. Mix on low, increasing speed as mixture softens. Mix until evenly blended. Pour mixture into crust and smooth the top. Freeze pie for at least 90 minutes.

Remove pie from freezer about 30 minutes before serving and cover with topping.

For topping: In a bowl, combine sour cream and maple syrup. Spread topping over pie in pretty swirls and decorate with pecans.

Makes 10 servings.

Caramel Apple Crumb Pie

Never miss an opportunity to combine caramel and apples—a flavor combination made in heaven. In bygone days, apple pie this good was grounds for a marriage proposal. Bake with caution!

Basic Pie Pastry (recipe on page 185)

TOPPING:

¾ cup all-purpose flour

½ cup old-fashioned rolled oats

½ cup packed brown sugar

¼ teaspoon ground cinnamon

⅛ teaspoon salt

6 tablespoons (¾ stick) cold, unsalted butter, cut into ¼-inch pieces

FILLING:

8 cups peeled, cored, and sliced baking apples

⅓ cup plus 1 tablespoon sugar, divided

1 tablespoon fresh lemon juice

2 tablespoons cornstarch

⅛ teaspoon salt

CARAMEL SAUCE:

½ cup heavy cream

⅓ cup packed brown sugar

2 tablespoons (¼ stick) unsalted butter, in pieces

½ teaspoon vanilla extract

½ cup chopped pecans

For crust: Roll refrigerated pie pastry dough into a 13-inch circle and line a 9½-inch deep-dish pie plate with it. Pinch overhanging pastry into an upstanding rim. Refrigerate for 15 minutes.

For topping: In a food processor, combine flour, oats, brown sugar, cinnamon, and salt. Pulse several times to mix. Scatter butter pieces over mixture and pulse until it reaches a sandlike consistency. Transfer topping to a bowl and rub well with your fingers until texture is uniform. Refrigerate topping.

For filling: Adjust oven rack to center position and preheat oven to 375°F.

In a bowl, combine apples, ⅓ cup sugar, and lemon juice. Set aside for 10 minutes.

In a separate bowl, combine cornstarch and salt with remaining 1 tablespoon sugar and mix to blend. Add mixture to apples and stir. Pour apple filling into chilled piecrust, shaping apples into a smooth mound.

Bake for 35 minutes. Remove pie from oven. Spread topping evenly over filling and tamp down lightly to compact. Bake for 25 to 35 minutes more, or until juices bubble thickly around edge. Transfer to a cooling rack and let cool for at least 1 hour before serving.

For Caramel Sauce: In a saucepan, combine cream, brown sugar, and butter. Bring to a boil and cook for 2 minutes, whisking constantly. Remove from heat, add vanilla and pecans, and stir. Transfer to a small bowl and cool completely. Refrigerate briefly for a thicker sauce.

Serve pie with sauce drizzled over each slice.

Makes 8 servings.

Hazelnut Shortcakes With Honeyed Pears

Shortcake is too good to be monopolized by strawberries. Here's a fall version that combines fresh pears, hazelnut-flavored shortcakes, and coffee whipped cream—a harmony of flavors.

BISCUITS:

⅔ cup whole hazelnuts

¼ cup sugar, plus extra for sprinkling

2 cups all-purpose flour

1½ teaspoons baking powder

½ teaspoon baking soda

½ teaspoon salt

6 tablespoons (¾ stick) cold, unsalted butter, cut into ¼-inch pieces

1 egg

½ cup milk

¼ cup plain yogurt or sour cream

FILLING:

4 large, ripe pears, peeled, cored, and thinly sliced

2 tablespoons fresh orange juice

1½ teaspoons grated orange zest

1½ tablespoons mild honey

TOPPING:

3 tablespoons sugar

1 teaspoon instant coffee powder

1 cup heavy cream

¼ teaspoon vanilla extract

For biscuits: Adjust oven rack to center position and preheat oven to 350°F. Spread hazelnuts on a baking sheet and toast in oven for 8 to 10 minutes, or until hazelnuts are fragrant and skins have blistered. Immediately transfer hazelnuts to a tea towel. Cover with half the towel, then rub briskly to remove skins. (Don't worry if a bit of skin remains.) Discard skins and set hazelnuts aside to cool.

Increase oven temperature to 400°F. Lightly butter a baking sheet or line with parchment paper.

In a food processor, combine hazelnuts with sugar. Pulse until hazelnuts are finely ground.

In a bowl, combine ground hazelnut mixture, flour, baking powder, baking soda, and salt, and whisk well. Use a pastry blender to cut butter into dry ingredients and mix until mixture resembles coarse, uniform crumbs. Set aside.

In a separate bowl, whisk egg until frothy. Add milk and yogurt and whisk to incorporate. Reserve 2 tablespoons of this mixture for glaze. Make a well in dry ingredients and add remaining mixture. Stir with a wooden spoon until evenly mixed.

Flour your hands and, using a large spoon, scoop a scant ½ cup of dough for each biscuit and gently shape into a ball. Make seven or eight balls, evenly spacing them on prepared baking sheet. Brush each biscuit with reserved egg mixture and sprinkle with sugar. Bake biscuits for 20 to 22 minutes, turning baking sheet about halfway through, until biscuits are a rich golden color. Transfer biscuits to a cooling rack.

For filling: In a bowl, combine sliced pears, orange juice, orange zest, and honey. Stir gently, then refrigerate.

For topping: In a bowl, rub sugar and instant coffee powder together to combine. Set aside.

Using an electric hand or stand mixer and a chilled mixing bowl, beat cream until it starts to thicken. Add coffee-sugar and vanilla and continue to beat until cream holds soft peaks. Refrigerate if not using right away.

When you're ready to serve, cut biscuits in half. Cover each bottom biscuit half with some of the pears, add a big dollop of the coffee whipped cream, then crown with the top half of the biscuit.

Makes 7 or 8 servings.

Apple Cranberry Crisp

You'll enjoy the hint of cranberry tartness in this blushing fall fruit crisp. Keep in mind that cranberries are harvested only from late September through October and that the fresh fruit are available through late December, so make this crisp as soon as you see the deep-red berries available at your market.

FILLING:

6 cups peeled, cored, and sliced apples

2 cups fresh cranberries

⅔ cup sugar

2 tablespoons all-purpose flour

2 teaspoons fresh lemon juice

2 teaspoons grated orange zest

TOPPING:

1¼ cups all-purpose flour

¾ cup brown sugar

½ teaspoon ground cinnamon

¼ teaspoon salt

8 tablespoons (1 stick) cold, unsalted butter, cut into ¼-inch pieces

Adjust oven rack to center position and preheat oven to 350°F. Butter a 9x9-inch baking dish.

For filling: In a bowl, combine apples, cranberries, sugar, flour, lemon juice, and orange zest. Set aside for 10 minutes, stirring occasionally.

For topping: In a food processor, combine flour, brown sugar, cinnamon, and salt and pulse briefly to mix. Scatter butter over dry mixture. Pulse several times, or until it has a sandlike consistency. Transfer topping mixture to a bowl and rub mixture between your fingers until it is uniform and clumpy.

Spread fruit mixture in prepared pan, then sprinkle with topping. Bake for 45 minutes, or until apples are soft and cranberries are bubbly. Set pan on a cooling rack for at least 10 minutes before serving.

Makes 8 servings.

Winter Recipes

Winter cooking runs the gamut from simple comfort food to elaborate entertaining. It's the perfect time of year to slow down and savor all that you have preserved from the growing season. While you may have very little, or possibly nothing, coming fresh from the garden during the winter months, plenty of late-fall vegetables are still available. If you have a root cellar or a local winter farmers' market, you likely have access to stored harvests— including beets, winter squashes, apples, potatoes, cabbages, and more. And let's not forget about citrus! Even if you live in a region where citrus trees are not productive, many varieties of oranges and grapefruit are widely available at this time of year and can be used to liven up everything from pork chops to cake. So head inside, heat up the oven, and enjoy the soups, roasts, and baked treats that can brighten up these short days and chilly nights.

Harvest Squash Rolls

These rolls are divine and worth the triple rise time. Try pairing with Herb Butter (recipe on page 97) to enhance the flavor even more. Note that this recipe makes enough rolls for a large crowd.

4 tablespoons active dry yeast

1 cup lukewarm (105° to 115°F) water

1⅓ cups vegetable shortening

1 cup sugar

4 eggs

2 cups cooked and mashed winter
    squash

2 cups warm milk

8 cups all-purpose flour, plus more
    as needed

2 teaspoons salt

 FUN FACT: Some of the most popular types of winter squashes include buttercups, hubbards, butternuts, acorns, and pumpkins. Many of the hard-rinded winter squashes will keep 6 months or more if free from injury, properly cured, and stored in a cool (50° to 55°F), dry space.

In a bowl, dissolve yeast in warm water. Set aside until foamy.

Using an electric hand or stand mixer, cream shortening with sugar. Beat in eggs. Add squash and mix until blended. Add warm milk and yeast mixture. Slowly add flour and salt. Continue to mix until dough pulls away from side of bowl, adding additional flour (in small amounts) as needed to make a soft dough. Let dough rise, covered, until doubled in size. Punch down, cover, then let rise again until doubled.

Preheat oven to 375°F. Grease four 9-inch cake pans.

Divide dough into four equal pieces, then divide each quarter into 12 pieces. Shape each piece into a ball.

Place balls in a single layer, touching, in prepared pans. Cover and let rise until doubled. Bake for 20 minutes, or until lightly browned. Remove from pans and set aside to cool.

Makes 4 dozen rolls.

Two-Cabbage Slaw

The colorful combination of red and green cabbage, plus the piquant flavor of horseradish, make this an exceptional salad. Be sure to make this slaw several hours ahead of serving time so that there's plenty of time for the flavors to come alive.

½ cup mayonnaise

2 tablespoons fresh lemon juice

2 tablespoons apple cider vinegar

2 tablespoons vegetable or olive oil

2 tablespoons sugar

2 tablespoons horseradish

1 teaspoon salt

1 teaspoon celery seed

¼ teaspoon freshly ground black pepper

½ head green cabbage, shredded

½ head red cabbage, shredded

In a jar, combine mayonnaise, lemon juice, vinegar, oil, sugar, horseradish, salt, celery seed, and pepper and shake well.

Put cabbages in a bowl and pour in dressing; toss to mix. Cover bowl and let stand in a cool place for several hours to allow flavors to blend.

Makes 6 servings.

FUN FACT: Cabbage is, quite literally, the head of the *Brassica* family (which includes broccoli, cauliflower, brussels sprouts, and kale). The English word "cabbage" comes from the Latin word for "head" (*caput*).

Beet and Fennel Salad With Citrus Vinaigrette

The earthy taste of roasted beet pairs nicely with the faintly sweet taste of fennel in this wholesome green salad.

1 large beet, stem and greens removed

2 oranges

¼ cup white balsamic vinegar

2 teaspoons grated orange zest

1 to 2 teaspoons grated lemon zest

1 teaspoon Dijon-style mustard

½ teaspoon salt

¼ teaspoon freshly ground black pepper

¾ cup extra-virgin olive oil

4 cups mixed greens

1 bulb fennel, thinly sliced

6 ounces chèvre, crumbled, divided

Preheat oven to 400°F.

Wrap beet in foil and bake for 45 to 60 minutes, or until easily pierced with a knife. Cool until safe to handle, then wrap in a paper towel and rub to remove skin. Cut beet into quarters, then cut each quarter into 8 thin slices from root end to stem end; set aside.

Peel oranges, removing as much of the bitter white pith as possible. Then, holding the fruit over a bowl, use a sharp paring knife to cut out the fleshy segments. Reserve juice.

In a separate bowl, combine vinegar, orange zest, lemon zest, mustard, salt, pepper, and ¼ cup reserved orange juice. Slowly drizzle in oil, whisking continuously. Check seasonings and adjust to taste.

In another bowl, mix greens together with orange segments, beets, and fennel; toss with ½ cup of vinaigrette. Taste and add more vinaigrette, if desired. Divide salad mixture evenly among four plates. Top each salad with chèvre immediately before serving.

Makes 4 servings.

Chai-Spiced Orange-Cranberry Sauce

A gentle hint of chai tea lends warm spice flavors to this sweetly aromatic, simple sauce. Pay close attention to the timing, though: Too much steeping will bring out the tea's bitter notes.

2¼ cups sugar

5 bags black chai tea

8 cups fresh or thawed frozen cranberries

¼ cup fresh orange juice

 FUN FACTS: The cranberry is native to North America. It's a member of the heath family and a relative of the blueberry and huckleberry. The Pilgrims and those who followed appreciated the wild berries but did not start to cultivate them until 1816, when a bog was planted and tended in Dennis, Massachusetts, on Cape Cod. By then, American and Canadian sailors on long voyages knew that they could eat cranberries to protect themselves from scurvy—making them a cranberry counterpart to "limeys," the British tars who sucked limes for the same purpose.

In a pot over high heat, combine sugar and 1½ cups water. Cover and bring to a boil, then reduce heat to medium-low and add tea bags. Simmer for exactly 2 minutes, then remove tea bags with a slotted spoon. Increase heat to medium-high and stir in cranberries. Simmer, stirring often, for 10 to 15 minutes, or until cranberries soften and split their skins and sauce thickens a bit. Remove from heat and stir in orange juice. Let cool to room temperature before serving or cover and refrigerate for up to 5 days. The sauce will thicken as it cools.

Makes 6 cups.

Maple-Orange-Glazed Vegetables

This easy glaze can be added to a variety of vegetables. It's delicious not only with the carrots and parsnips suggested here, but also with baked squash—just brush it on during the last few minutes of cooking.

4 to 6 large carrots or parsnips, peeled and cut into thick slices

1 tablespoon butter

¼ cup maple syrup

2 tablespoons frozen orange juice concentrate

pinch of salt

pinch of ground nutmeg

chopped walnuts, for garnish

Bring a pot of salted water to a boil. Add carrots and cook until tender but still firm. Drain and set aside.

In a skillet over medium heat, melt butter. Add maple syrup, orange juice concentrate, salt, and nutmeg and stir to combine. Add carrots and stir for about 2 minutes, or until all carrots are glazed. Garnish with chopped walnuts. Serve immediately.

Makes 4 to 6 servings.

STORAGE TIPS:
• Carrots, beets, parsnips, and other root crops should be brushed clean of any soil and stored in a cool, dark place such as a dry basement.

* Clipping the tops off carrots, beets, parsnips, and turnips will keep them fresher longer.

* Store root crops in layers of sand and peat in polyethylene bags with breathing holes and keep them in the lowest area of the basement or cellar.

Winter Vegetable Curry

This spicy dish is a good choice for a night when you need to toss supper together in a hurry. Serve it with rice and chutney.

3 tablespoons vegetable oil

3 cloves garlic, finely chopped

1 onion, finely chopped

1 tablespoon grated fresh ginger

1 teaspoon ground cumin

1 teaspoon cayenne pepper

1 teaspoon chili powder

½ teaspoon ground cardamom

1 green bell pepper, finely chopped

2 carrots, finely chopped

2 parsnips, finely chopped

1 tart apple, peeled, cored,
    and chopped

1 cup fresh orange juice

2 tablespoons raisins

salt and freshly ground black pepper,
    to taste

In a skillet over low heat, warm oil. Add garlic, onions, ginger, cumin, cayenne, chili powder, and cardamom and cook, stirring, until onions are soft. Increase heat to medium and add bell peppers, carrots, parsnips, apples, orange juice, and raisins; stir to combine and cook for about 15 minutes, or until the vegetables are tender. Season with salt and pepper.

Makes 6 servings.

FUN FACT: Did you know you that you can grow ginger at home? Simply take a fresh ginger rhizome and break off a piece about 2 inches long. Plant it in sandy soil and water occasionally, keeping it slightly moistened. In 4 to 5 weeks, the root will start to grow and you can break off a piece as needed. The root will continue to grow.

Latkes

Latkes are shallow-fried pancakes made with grated potatoes, flour, and egg, often enjoyed with sour cream or applesauce. These latkes pair nicely with Cinnamon Applesauce (recipe on page 93).

4 russet potatoes, peeled and grated

1 onion, grated

1 egg, lightly beaten

2 tablespoons all-purpose flour

1 teaspoon kosher or sea salt, plus extra for seasoning

½ teaspoon baking powder

vegetable oil, for frying

freshly ground black pepper, to taste

sour cream or applesauce, for serving

fresh chives, for garnish

Place potatoes and onions in a sieve or kitchen towel and squeeze out excess water.

In a bowl, combine potatoes, onions, egg, flour, salt, and baking powder. Stir until everything is evenly coated.

In a heavy skillet over medium heat, warm a thin layer of oil (about 2 tablespoons). Drop batter into skillet one heaping spoonful at a time, but don't crowd the pan. Flatten gently; don't push potatoes too hard into oil. (Each latke should be about 2 inches wide.) Fry in batches, 4 minutes per side, or until golden brown, turning once. Add more oil as needed to skillet for additional batches to prevent sticking. Drain on paper towels and season well with salt and pepper. Serve warm with a dollop of sour cream and garnish with chives.

Makes 12 servings.

Braised Red Cabbage With Apples

This classic sweet-and-sour side dish is highly adaptable to your personal tastes through the addition of a little more vinegar or a little more sugar to match your mood. The vibrant color and flavor are perfect paired with roasted turkey or pork.

1 red cabbage, shredded

7 tablespoons salted butter

2 onions, diced

6 apples, peeled, cored, and diced

4 cloves garlic, minced

2 cups apple cider

6 whole cloves

4 bay leaves

1 cinnamon stick

1 teaspoon kosher or sea salt

1 teaspoon freshly ground black pepper

3 tablespoons brown sugar, plus extra to taste

3 tablespoons apple cider vinegar, plus extra to taste

1 heaping tablespoon cornstarch

In a bowl, soak cabbage in cold water for 1 hour. (This step is optional, but it does take away the bitterness.) Strain through a colander.

Preheat oven to 350°F.

In a Dutch oven over medium-high heat, melt butter. When butter sizzles, add onions and cook for about 6 minutes, or until clear. Add apples and garlic and stir for 1 minute. Add cabbage, cider, cloves, bay leaves, cinnamon stick, salt, and pepper; stir well. Cover and bake for about 1½ hours, or until very tender.

In a bowl, whisk together brown sugar, vinegar, and cornstarch. Remove cabbage from oven and put over low heat. Slowly add vinegar mixture while stirring and cook for about 3 minutes, or until sauce thickens. Taste sauce and add extra sugar or vinegar, to taste. Remove bay leaves and cinnamon stick before serving.

Makes 8 to 10 servings.

HARVEST TIPS:
• Harvest cabbage heads when they have reached desired size and are firm. Most early varieties will produce 1- to 3-pound heads.

* Cut each cabbage head at its base with a sharp knife. After harvesting, bring inside or place in shade immediately.

* Cabbage can be stored in the refrigerator for no more than 2 weeks, wrapped lightly in plastic. Make sure that it is dry before storing. In proper root cellar conditions, cabbage will keep for up to 3 months.

Cabbage Gratin

This baked cabbage dish is a wonderful way to enjoy this hardy,
leafy vegetable that is chock-full of vitamins. Cabbage stores well and
is loaded with vitamins C and K, beta-carotene, and fiber, so it may
be just what you need to bolster your health this winter.

2 tablespoons unsalted butter

1 tablespoon vegetable oil

1 head cabbage, quartered and sliced
    into ½-inch-wide pieces

2 scallions, chopped

2 carrots, grated

salt and freshly ground black pepper,
    to taste

1½ cups chicken stock

8 ounces grated Parmesan cheese

Heat oven to 350°F. Grease a 2-quart casserole.

In a skillet over medium heat, melt butter with oil. Add
cabbage, scallions, and carrots and stir to combine.
Season generously with salt and pepper and cook,
stirring, for 10 minutes, or until cabbage is nicely
wilted and just beginning to brown in spots. Add
stock and adjust heat to a simmer; cook for about 5
minutes. Transfer mixture to casserole, cover tightly
with foil, and bake for 30 minutes. Remove foil and
continue to bake for 20 minutes more, or until liquid
is mostly evaporated. Remove dish from oven, sprinkle
with Parmesan, and increase oven to 375°F. Return
dish to oven and bake for 10 minutes, or until cheese
is thoroughly melted. You can serve the dish at this
point, but for extra deliciousness, place casserole under
broiler for 2 minutes immediately before serving.

Makes 6 to 8 servings.

Butternut Squash Soup

The addition of maple syrup at the end of cooking time brings a subtle sweetness to this soup and works to accentuate the butternut flavor.

3 tablespoons butter

1 carrot, peeled and chopped

2 tablespoons chopped onions

3 tablespoons all-purpose flour

4 cups warm chicken stock

2 pounds butternut squash, peeled, seeded, and cut into large cubes

1 clove garlic

1 tablespoon dried parsley

1½ cups milk

½ cup light cream

2 tablespoons maple syrup, or to taste

freshly ground black pepper, to taste

pumpkin seeds, for garnish

FUN FACTS: Winter squash is a nutritional powerhouse, a superior source of vitamin A, and a good source of fiber, vitamin C, the B complex vitamins, potassium, and many other essential minerals. In addition, winter squash contains unusually high amounts of several carotenoids, a class of pigments that give many fruit and vegetables their orange or yellow tinge. Although most of its calories come from carbohydrates, winter squash contains a special class of carbohydrates that have anti-inflammatory, antioxidant, and cholesterol- and insulin-regulating properties.

In a pot over medium-low heat, melt butter. Add carrots and onions and cook for about 5 minutes, or until onions are tender. Sprinkle vegetables with flour and, stirring constantly, continue cooking for 3 minutes. Add chicken stock and stir to combine. Add squash, garlic, and parsley and simmer, covered, for 45 minutes. Remove from heat and set aside to cool for 10 minutes.

In a blender or food processor, purée soup, in batches, until smooth. Return soup to pot, add milk, cream, and syrup, and stir to incorporate and heat through. Season with pepper and garnish with pumpkin seeds.

Make ahead: This soup can be prepared up to the purée stage, covered, and refrigerated for 4 days or frozen in an airtight container for 1 month. To serve from refrigerated or frozen: For each serving, combine ½ cup of the thawed purée, 2 tablespoons of milk, 2 teaspoons of cream, and 1 teaspoon of maple syrup, then heat through.

Makes 12 servings.

Roasted Brussels Sprouts With Shallots and Bacon

Brussels sprouts, a member of the cabbage family, seem to have been making a culinary comeback in recent years. If you're not yet convinced of their tastiness, this could be the recipe to help you join the ranks of those who can't get enough of these little cabbages.

6 slices thick-cut bacon, cut into ½-inch pieces

2½ pounds small brussels sprouts, ends trimmed and halved lengthwise

8 shallots, halved lengthwise

2 teaspoons kosher or sea salt

1 teaspoon freshly ground black pepper

1 to 2 tablespoons olive oil or vegetable oil

1 cup pecan halves

½ cup dry white wine or chicken stock

Preheat oven to 400°F.

In an ovenproof skillet over medium heat, cook bacon, stirring often, for 6 to 8 minutes, or until it begins to brown. Add brussels sprouts, shallots, salt, and pepper, and stir. If pan looks dry, add oil. Cook, stirring continuously, for 5 minutes, or until brussels sprouts begin to turn golden. Stir in pecans and transfer pan to oven. Cook for 15 to 20 minutes, or until vegetables are tender. Remove from oven, add wine, and stir to pick up any browned bits from the bottom of the pan. Serve warm.

Makes 10 servings.

 GROWING TIPS: Brussels sprouts have a long growing season and are generally more successful when grown for a late fall harvest, as they increase in flavor after a light frost or two. You can even harvest them into the winter if you provide a cover or protect the plant by mulching with straw.

Swiss Chard and Pasta Soup With Turkey Meatballs

If you're new to eating Swiss chard, try this soup. It's the perfect way to consume a good amount of this powerfully healthy green. As with all leafy greens, the chard will shrink considerably when cooked, so don't balk at adding all 5 cups.

1 egg

1 pound lean ground turkey

1¼ cups plain bread crumbs

⅓ cup freshly grated Parmesan cheese, plus more for garnish

2 tablespoons finely chopped fresh parsley

2 cloves garlic, minced

1 teaspoon kosher or sea salt, plus extra to taste

freshly ground black pepper, to taste

8 cups low-sodium chicken stock

2 carrots, peeled and diced

1 cup penne pasta

5 cups white Swiss chard (or escarole), stems trimmed, washed, and coarsely chopped

1 cup shredded mozzarella

In a bowl, whisk egg and 2 tablespoons of water together. Add turkey, bread crumbs, Parmesan, parsley, garlic, salt, and pepper. With moistened hands, shape turkey mixture into meatballs. Place on a baking sheet and chill for 30 minutes.

In a pot over high heat, bring chicken stock to a boil. Reduce heat to medium and add carrots and meatballs; simmer for 8 minutes. Add pasta and cook for about 3 minutes, or al dente. Stir in chard and simmer for about 3 to 5 minutes, or until tender. Season with salt and pepper. Divide mozzarella into six serving bowls and ladle soup into bowls. Garnish with additional Parmesan.

Makes 6 servings.

PLANTING TIP: Swiss chard seeds should be soaked in water for at least 24 hours before planting. Each seed is actually a dried fruit with one to five seeds in it. Most will sprout, so it's important to thin seedlings to at least 12 inches apart so that plants can grow vigorously.

Kale, Sausage, and White Bean Soup

Although this soup is fantastic as is, it's also very adaptable to substitutions and additions. If you want to add color and sweetness, substitute diced winter squash for potato. Or, add cooked pasta at the end to make a minestrone.

½ pound fresh kale

3 to 4 links hot or mild Italian sausage

3 tablespoons olive oil

1 onion, chopped

1 stalk celery, chopped

1 carrot, peeled and chopped

2 cloves garlic, minced

3 cups chicken stock

1 russet potato, peeled and diced

1 can (14 ounces) diced tomatoes, with juice

2 tablespoons tomato paste

1 teaspoon salt, plus more to taste

1 teaspoon dried basil

½ teaspoon dried thyme

freshly ground black pepper, to taste

1 can (15 or 19 ounces) cannellini beans, drained and rinsed

finely grated Parmesan cheese, for topping

Strip kale leaves from stems and tear leaves into large pieces. Discard stems. Rinse kale in a bowl of cool water, then transfer to a colander and set aside.

Bring a large pot of water to a boil. Pierce each sausage link several times with a paring knife, place in boiling water, and cook for 10 minutes. Transfer to a plate until cool enough to handle, then remove casings and cut links into ¼-inch-thick slices.

In a pot over medium heat, warm oil. Add onions, celery, and carrots and cook for 5 minutes, or until onions are soft. Add garlic and cook for 1 minute more. Add 3 cups of water, stock, kale, and sausage. Bring to a simmer, stirring occasionally. Add potatoes, tomatoes with juice, tomato paste, salt, basil, thyme, and pepper and simmer for 20 to 25 minutes, or until kale is tender. Add beans and simmer for 5 to 10 minutes more. Taste and adjust seasonings. Serve hot and pass Parmesan at the table.

Makes 8 or more servings.

GROWING TIP: Dark leafy greens, including kale, can withstand quite a bit of cold. Depending on your climate, you may be able to grow these hardy and nutritious greens into the winter. Cold frames or even a fairly simple hoop and plastic system of coverage might keep you in kale well past your area's first frost date.

Orange-Glazed Sweet Potatoes

This lively-tasting orange glaze is also great over grilled ham
steaks or chicken. To save time, make the sauce a few days
ahead and refrigerate it until you're ready to use it.

6 sweet potatoes

3 tablespoons butter

1 tablespoon cornstarch

1 cup fresh orange juice

⅓ cup sugar

⅓ cup brown sugar

pinch of salt

HARVEST TIPS:
• After digging up sweet
potatoes, shake off any
excess dirt but do not wash
the roots.

* You must cure sweet potatoes
in order for them to acquire
their sweet taste. Curing the
potatoes allows a second skin to
form over scratches and bruises
that occur when digging up the
potatoes. To cure, keep the roots
in a warm place (about 80°F) at
high humidity (about 90 percent)
for 10 to 14 days. A table outside
in a shady spot works well. For
best curing, make sure that the
potatoes are not touching one
another.

Bring a pot of salted water to a boil. Add sweet potatoes
and cook for 30 minutes. Remove sweet potatoes from
water, peel, and slice in half lengthwise. Place sweet
potato slices in a casserole and set aside.

Preheat oven to 350°F.

In a saucepan over medium heat, melt butter. Add
cornstarch and stir until dissolved and smooth. Add
orange juice, stirring constantly. Add sugars and salt,
then cook, stirring constantly, until sauce is thickened.
Pour sauce over sweet potatoes in casserole and bake
for 30 minutes. Serve hot.

Makes 6 servings.

Roast Leg of Lamb With Potatoes and Rutabaga

This winter roast is simple, classic, and sure to please. Allow 1 pound of lamb per serving if roast is bone-in and closer to ½ pound per person if roast is boneless. Because bones conduct heat, you'll need to add a little additional cooking time if the roast is boneless.

1 leg of lamb (5 to 6 pounds)

2 to 3 cloves garlic, slivered

1 tablespoon Dijon-style mustard

freshly ground black pepper

4 to 6 russet potatoes, peeled and quartered

1 rutabaga, peeled and cut into wedges

ROASTING TIPS:
• Remove the roast from the refrigerator up to 2 hours before you put it into the oven. This gives it a chance to warm up to room temperature and cook evenly.

• Make sure that the oven is preheated before you put the roast in.

• Always use a meat thermometer—preferably the instant-read type—inserted into the thickest part of the flesh, away from bone, fat, and gristle.

• Before carving, let the roast rest for at least 20 minutes after you remove it from the oven to allow the reabsorption of juices.

Preheat oven to 500°F. Get out a roasting pan.

Make slits in lamb and insert slivers of garlic. Rub lamb with mustard and season generously with pepper. Place lamb in roasting pan and cook for 20 minutes. Reduce oven temperature to 350°F and remove pan from oven. Add potatoes and rutabaga around lamb and coat vegetables with pan drippings. Return to oven for 50 to 70 minutes (depending on the bone), or until an instant-read thermometer reads 145°F for medium-rare or 160°F for medium, basting occasionally with pan juices.

Makes 6 servings.

Potato and Broccoli Soup

This is a creamy, warming, and filling soup that is easily altered to taste.
If your stock isn't as flavorful as you'd like, feel free to add some additional
flavors (such as garlic and onions) as you make this soup.

4 cups peeled and diced potatoes

2 cups chicken stock

1 head broccoli, stalks removed,
 roughly chopped

1 cup milk

1 cup light cream

1 cup shredded cheddar cheese

salt and freshly ground black pepper,
 to taste

1 tablespoon butter (optional)

 FUN FACT: Properly cured
and stored potatoes will
typically last in a root cellar
through April, which makes
them a readily available
treat throughout the entire winter.

In a pot of lightly salted water over high heat, cook potatoes, covered, for 10 to 15 minutes, or until tender. Drain and set aside.

In the same pot over medium heat, combine chicken stock and broccoli. Cook, covered, for about 10 minutes, or until broccoli is very tender. Remove from heat. Using a large spoon, chop the broccoli into fairly small pieces against the side of the pot.

Place about 1 cup of cooked potatoes on a plate and mash well with a fork. Add mashed potatoes and remaining chopped potatoes to broccoli mixture, then add milk and cream. Heat gently until hot but not boiling. Add cheddar and stir gently until melted and well blended. Season with salt and pepper and stir in butter (if using).

Makes 4 to 6 servings.

Broccoli and Cheddar Strata

Serve this savory bread pudding as a brunch dish for a crowd. Almost all of the preparation for this dish can be done in advance (even the night before), so all you have to do in the morning is put it in the oven.

5 tablespoons unsalted butter, divided

1 large loaf soft French or Italian bread, crust removed, cut into 1-inch cubes

1 onion, chopped

2 cups bite-size broccoli florets

1 cup diced smoked sausage

1 clove garlic, minced

6 eggs

2½ cups half-and-half or milk

2 teaspoons Dijon-style mustard

1 teaspoon dried basil

¾ teaspoon salt

¼ teaspoon freshly ground black pepper

2 cups shredded sharp cheddar cheese

Butter a 13x9-inch casserole or six to eight individual ramekins lavishly with 2 tablespoons of butter. Add bread cubes to cover bottom of casserole(s).

In a skillet over medium heat, melt remaining 3 tablespoons of butter. Add onions and cook for 5 minutes, or until soft. Add broccoli, sausage, and garlic and cook for 3 minutes more, or until broccoli is soft. Remove skillet from heat and spoon broccoli mixture over bread in casserole.

In a bowl, whisk eggs lightly. Add half-and-half, mustard, basil, salt, and pepper and whisk to blend. Ladle or pour egg mixture over ingredients in casserole. Press gently with a fork or spoon to moisten all of the bread. Sprinkle with cheddar, cover with plastic wrap, and refrigerate for at least 2 hours or overnight.

Preheat oven to 350°F. Remove plastic wrap and bake small casseroles for 25 to 30 minutes or single large casserole for 45 to 55 minutes, or until a knife inserted into the center comes out clean. Transfer to a cooling rack for 10 minutes before serving.

Makes 10 to 12 servings.

Orange Pork Chops

The citrus in this recipe really jazzes up the pork chops, adding
a welcome zing to a winter meal. Serve with a side of rice
or your favorite starch for full comfort food mode.

4 thick pork chops

1 clove garlic, halved

zest of 1 orange

1 cup fresh orange juice

1 cup sour cream, room temperature

HARVEST TIPS:
* Depending on the climate, citrus fruit may take 6 to 8 months to ripen.

* Citrus fruit will not ripen off the tree, so refrain from picking them too early. The best indicator of ripeness is taste.

* Undamaged citrus fruit can be stored for several weeks at cool temperatures.

Preheat oven to 350°F. Get out a covered casserole.

Rub pork chops with cut sides of garlic. Trim fat and rub it over cooking surface of a skillet. Place skillet over medium heat and brown chops. Place browned chops in casserole. Sprinkle orange zest over chops and add juice to casserole. Bake for 1 hour, or until a thermometer inserted into thickest portion of chops reads 145°F.

Before serving, mix sour cream with juices in casserole.

Makes 4 servings.

Orange-Almond Chicken

This simple method of preparing chicken makes use of ingredients that you likely already have on hand. The featured orange gravy brightens the flavors, and the toasted almonds add an additional crunch.

1 teaspoon paprika

1 teaspoon salt

¼ teaspoon freshly ground black pepper

1 fryer chicken (about 3 pounds), cut up

⅓ cup butter

1 cup fresh orange juice

⅔ cup toasted slivered almonds

1 teaspoon cornstarch (optional)

Preheat oven to 200°F or to a "keep warm" setting. Put an ovenproof platter in the oven as it preheats.

In a resealable plastic bag, combine paprika, salt, and pepper and shake to mix. Add chicken to bag, seal, and shake until thoroughly coated.

In a skillet over medium heat, melt butter. Sauté chicken pieces until golden brown on all sides. Cover skillet, reduce heat, and cook for 25 to 30 minutes, or until chicken is done. Remove chicken to warm platter and keep in oven.

Pour orange juice into skillet and increase heat to high. Stir and scrape to loosen all of the browned bits. Cook until juice is reduced by half. Remove chicken from oven and pour reduced orange juice over chicken. Sprinkle with toasted almonds and serve at once. If you prefer a thicker gravy, blend cornstarch with 1 teaspoon of water; stir mixture into the reduced orange juice and cook until thickened.

Makes 4 servings.

Stuffed Mashed Potatoes

This is a fun twist on traditional mashed potatoes. A crunchy topping, melted mozzarella, and savory bits of pepperoni make this the ultimate comfort food.

2 pounds russet potatoes, scrubbed

¼ cup (½ stick) butter

½ teaspoon salt

½ teaspoon garlic powder

¼ teaspoon freshly ground black pepper

½ pound mozzarella cheese, cut into 12 pieces

3 ounces pepperoni, finely chopped

3 tablespoons seasoned bread crumbs

Preheat oven to 400°F. Using a fork, poke holes in potatoes, then place on baking sheet. Bake for 45 to 55 minutes, or until tender. Remove potatoes from oven. Do not turn off oven. Grease a 12-cup muffin tin.

Peel potatoes while still hot, then put through a ricer or shred using a grater over a bowl. Add butter, salt, garlic powder, and pepper and mix until butter has melted. Fill each muffin cup about halfway with potato mixture. Place 1 piece of mozzarella in each cup. Divide pepperoni evenly between cups. Top with remaining potatoes. Sprinkle bread crumbs over each. Return to oven and bake for 10 to 12 minutes. Unmold immediately and serve.

Makes 12 servings.

Sweet Potato and Sausage Casserole

This crowd-pleasing casserole is a perfect dish to take along for sharing.
Just sprinkle with cheese and heat it up before serving.

6 large sweet potatoes, peeled
and quartered

butter, to taste

salt and freshly ground black pepper,
to taste

1 pound Italian sweet sausage,
casings removed

2 cups diced fresh mushrooms

1 sweet onion, diced

4 apples, peeled, cored, and thinly
sliced

1 cup shredded cheddar cheese

 FUN FACTS: Sweet
potatoes (*Ipomoea
batatas*) are not related
to regular white potatoes,
belonging instead to
the morning glory family—
Convolvulaceae. Their heart-shape
leaves are a reminder of that
relationship. They are not a tuber
but a fleshy root native to Central
and South America. Depending on
the variety, they can have dry or
moist flesh in colors ranging from
white to yellow, orange, red, and
even purple.

Preheat oven to 350°F. Grease a 13x9-inch casserole.

Put sweet potatoes in a pot, cover with water, and bring
to a boil. Reduce heat and simmer for 20 minutes, or
until potatoes are fork-tender. Drain, then add butter,
salt, and pepper. Mash sweet potatoes and set aside.

In a skillet over medium heat, break up sausage
and cook until no longer pink. Drain, reserving 2
tablespoons of fat. Transfer sausage to a bowl.

Return skillet to heat. Add reserved fat, mushrooms, and
onions and cook until onions are soft. Add mushrooms
and onions to bowl with sausage.

In prepared casserole, layer half the sweet potato
mixture, half the sausage mixture, and all of the apple
slices. Repeat, ending with sausage. Bake for 35 minutes.
Sprinkle with cheddar and bake for 10 minutes more.

Makes 6 to 8 servings.

Pork Tenderloin With Apples and Red Cabbage

This pork tenderloin dish with apples and red cabbage is as flavorful as it is attractive. If you don't have red currant jelly, you can substitute cranberry sauce, sour cherry jam, or not-too-sweet Concord grape jam.

2 tart apples, peeled, cored, and sliced

2 teaspoons lemon juice

5 tablespoons vegetable oil, divided

1 pound boneless pork tenderloin, cut into thin strips

2 onions, thinly sliced

1 head red cabbage, finely shredded

1 cup unsweetened apple juice

¼ cup red currant jelly

3 tablespoons red-wine vinegar

¼ teaspoon ground allspice

salt and freshly ground black pepper, to taste

In a bowl, toss apples with lemon juice and set aside.

In a heavy skillet over medium heat, warm 3 tablespoons of oil. Cook pork for 4 to 5 minutes, or until done, then remove from skillet and drain on paper towels.

Warm remaining 2 tablespoons of oil in skillet. Cook onions until soft but not brown. Add cabbage and cook, stirring often, until it begins to wilt. Add apples and pork and stir to combine.

In a separate bowl, combine apple juice, jelly, vinegar, and allspice. Season with salt and pepper, then pour over mixture in skillet, stirring to coat. Cover and simmer for 10 to 15 minutes, checking to make sure that pan does not dry out. Add water if necessary.

Makes 4 to 6 servings.

Stuffed Acorn Squash

This simple, filling meal kicks it up a notch with a charming presentation, as each half of the acorn squash serves as its own bowl.

1 large acorn squash, halved and
    seeded

olive oil, to taste

salt and freshly ground black pepper,
    to taste

1 pound ground sausage

1 apple or pear, cored and diced

 TIP: When buying a winter squash, choose one that's heavy for its size, has a hard rind, and is free from soft spots. Don't worry about warts and brown ridges.

Preheat oven to 400°F. Line a baking sheet with aluminum foil.

Place squash, cut side up, on prepared baking sheet. Drizzle with olive oil and sprinkle with salt and pepper. Bake for 30 to 45 minutes, or until flesh is tender.

In a skillet over medium heat, brown sausage. When cooked thoroughly, add apples and stir until fruit is softened. Season with salt and pepper.

Stuff cooked squash cavities with sausage–apple mixture and bake for 10 to 15 minutes more. Cool slightly before serving.

Makes 2 servings.

Toffee Popcorn

This is a perfect treat for movie night or a cozy evening by the fire. It's especially fun if you grew your own popping corn (see tip below). Note: It takes about ½ cup of unpopped kernels to get 12 cups of popped corn.

12 cups popped popcorn

½ cup (1 stick) butter

¾ cup packed brown sugar

¼ cup honey

pinch of salt

1 teaspoon vanilla extract

⅓ cup toffee bits

PLANTING AND HARVESTING TIPS:

• Plant seed popcorn in four or five short rows about 36 inches apart to ensure pollination. Plant corn seeds 1 inch deep and 6 inches apart. When the plants are 5 inches tall, thin them to 12 inches apart.

• When the stalks are about knee-high, hill them up 6 inches by scraping soil from between the rows. Hilling adds nutrients and support to the growing plants.

• Let the husks that cover the ears turn brown before harvesting. If you can press your thumbnail into a kernel, it's not ripe yet.

• Harvest all ears before the first hard frost. Shuck the ears and let them dry for a few weeks, then shell the kernels and store them in airtight containers in the refrigerator.

Put popcorn into a bowl and discard any unpopped kernels.

In a saucepan over medium heat, combine butter, brown sugar, honey, and salt, stirring constantly. Bring to a simmer, whisk in vanilla, and simmer for 4 to 5 minutes. The longer this simmers, the crunchier the coating will be. Pour sauce over popcorn and gently toss until popcorn is evenly coated. Sprinkle with toffee bits and stir until evenly incorporated. Store in an airtight container.

Makes 12 cups.

Pound Cake With Grapefruit Glaze

This pound cake is a winter favorite, especially once you add the bright, sweet-tart flavor of the grapefruit glaze. You can use any variety of grapefruit here or substitute another citrus juice and adjust the sugar to taste.

CAKE:

3 cups cake flour (cooking tip below)

1½ teaspoons salt

1 teaspoon baking powder

1 cup (2 sticks) unsalted butter, softened

2 cups sugar

zest of 1 grapefruit

1¼ teaspoons grapefruit or lemon extract (optional)

4 eggs, at room temperature

½ cup fresh grapefruit juice

GLAZE:

1½ cups confectioners' sugar

2 to 3 tablespoons fresh grapefruit juice

COOKING TIP: If you don't have cake flour on hand, you can easily make your own using all-purpose flour and cornstarch. Here's the formula for homemade cake flour:

1 cup all-purpose flour – 2 tablespoons all-purpose flour + 2 tablespoons cornstarch = 1 cup cake flour

A simple way to achieve this is to measure the cornstarch into the cup measure first, then spoon in all-purpose flour to a level cup. Once you've measured the all-purpose flour and cornstarch to reach the total number of cups of cake flour required for your recipe, sift the mixture multiple times until the cornstarch is fully incorporated before using in a recipe as directed.

For cake: Preheat oven to 325°F. Mist a 10-inch Bundt or tube pan with nonstick cooking spray.

In a bowl, combine flour, salt, and baking powder.

Using an electric hand or stand mixer, cream butter until color lightens, about 2 minutes. Add sugar gradually, then beat for about 4 minutes, or until fluffy. Add grapefruit zest and extract (if using) and mix thoroughly. Add eggs, one at a time, beating well after each addition. Add one-third of the flour mixture, then beat until just incorporated. Add ¼ cup of grapefruit juice and another third of the flour mixture; beat until just incorporated. Repeat with remaining ¼ cup of grapefruit juice and remaining flour mixture.

Pour batter into prepared pan, tap pan on counter to get rid of any air pockets, and bake for 50 minutes, or until a toothpick inserted into the center comes out clean. Place on a cooling rack for 10 minutes. Loosen sides with a knife, then turn cake out of pan onto rack. Let cool for 45 minutes, or until it is at room temperature.

For glaze: In a bowl, combine sugar and juice and mix with a fork until smooth. With the cake still on the cooling rack, set a piece of wax paper under the cake, then slowly drizzle glaze over top of cake. Let cake cool completely before transferring to a platter. If not serving immediately, refrigerate overnight or up to several days, covered loosely with foil.

Makes 4 to 6 servings.

Cranberry, Cardamom, and Citrus Pinwheels

These special cookies are perfect for a holiday cookie swap or enjoying with a cup of tea. With tart cranberries, notes of citrus, savory cardamom, and rich butter, the broad flavor profile is a joy to experience.

1 cup (2 sticks) butter, softened

1¼ cups sugar

½ teaspoon baking powder

½ teaspoon salt

2 eggs

2 teaspoons grated orange zest

3 cups all-purpose flour

1 cup fresh cranberries

1 cup pecans or walnuts

¼ cup packed brown sugar

1½ teaspoons ground cardamom

1 teaspoon ground nutmeg

 FUN FACT: Cardamom, *Elettaria cardamomum*, is the fruit of a large perennial bush that grows wild in Sri Lanka and southern India and is now cultivated heavily in parts of Central America. It has been used in Scandinavia and India for baking and savory dishes for thousands of years. Its aroma is strong, and only a small amount of it is required to impart its slightly floral flavor.

Using an electric hand or stand mixer, beat butter on medium to high speed for 30 seconds. Add sugar, baking powder, and salt and beat until combined, scraping sides of bowl occasionally. Beat in eggs and orange zest until combined. Add flour and mix well. Divide dough in half, cover each portion with plastic wrap, and chill for about 1 hour.

In a blender or food processor, combine cranberries, nuts, brown sugar, cardamom, and nutmeg. Blend until cranberries and nuts are finely chopped. Set filling aside until dough is ready.

Place one portion of dough between pieces of parchment or wax paper and roll dough into a 10-inch square. Spread half of filling over dough to within ½ inch of edges. Slowly and carefully roll dough into a round log. Wrap filled dough log in parchment paper or plastic wrap. Repeat with remaining portion of dough and filling. Chill for several hours.

Preheat oven to 375°F. Get out a baking sheet.

When dough is chilled solid, cut logs into ¼-inch-thick slices. Place slices 2 inches apart on baking sheet. Bake for 8 to 10 minutes, or until edges are firm and bottoms are lightly browned. Let sit on baking sheet for 1 to 2 minutes before transferring to a cooling rack.

Makes about 40 cookies.

Citrus Tart

Orange and spice flavors combine perfectly in this luscious dessert. The gingersnap crust can be made in advance and frozen for up to 2 weeks, and the pastry cream filling can be made up to 8 hours ahead of serving. Sectioning the oranges takes extra time (about 15 minutes) but yields a far superior result.

CRUST:

6 tablespoons (¾ stick) butter, divided

40 gingersnap wafers

PASTRY CREAM:

½ cup sugar

¼ cup cornstarch

⅛ teaspoon salt

4 egg yolks, lightly beaten

2 cups whole milk

1 tablespoon butter

1 teaspoon vanilla extract

1 to 2 tablespoons grated orange zest

2 teaspoons Grand Marnier liqueur (optional)

TOPPING:

10 medium or 8 large navel oranges

½ cup orange marmalade

¼ teaspoon ground cinnamon

chopped fresh mint, for garnish

For crust: Preheat oven to 325°F. Use 1 tablespoon of butter to coat a 9½-inch tart pan with removable bottom. Get out a baking sheet.

Grind gingersnaps in a food processor until they're the texture of sand, then pour into a bowl. In a bowl in the microwave or in a saucepan over low heat, melt remaining 5 tablespoons of butter. Pour butter over gingersnap crumbs and use your hands to combine. Press gingersnap crumb mixture into the bottom and up the sides of prepared tart pan. Place pan on baking sheet and refrigerate for 20 minutes. Transfer to oven and bake for about 15 minutes, or until lightly browned. Cool completely.

For pastry cream: In a heavy saucepan, combine sugar, cornstarch, and salt. Gradually whisk in yolks and milk, then bring to a boil over medium heat, whisking constantly. Boil for 1 minute, or until thickened. While cream is still warm, stir in butter, vanilla, orange zest, and Grand Marnier (if using). Press plastic wrap against entire surface of cream and let cool to room temperature.

For topping: Slice top and bottom off each orange. Starting from the top and following the shape of the fruit, cut away all of the pith and peel. Holding the orange over a bowl, cut away each section from the membrane. You should be left with wedge-shaped slices of pure fruit and a bowl of juice (save it to drink at breakfast). Drain orange slices on paper towels. While slices are draining, heat marmalade in a saucepan until it is liquid. Remove from heat and put through a mesh strainer. Add cinnamon to marmalade liquid and set aside.

To assemble: Pour cooled pastry cream into tart shell and spread evenly. Lay orange slices sideways around tart, layering each successive row on top of the previous row. Brush fruit with marmalade glaze. Chill. This dessert is best when served within 6 to 8 hours of final assembly. Garnish with fresh mint before serving.

Makes 12 servings.

Lemon-Orange Pudding Cakes

These single-serving pudding cakes puff up like soufflés and never fail to make a great impression—however, they are too hot to eat immediately after baking. Show them off straight from the oven but serve them about 30 minutes later.

1¼ cups sugar, divided

3 tablespoons all-purpose flour

big pinch of salt

1 cup milk

4 eggs, separated, at room temperature

½ cup fresh orange juice

¼ cup fresh lemon juice

¼ cup (½ stick) unsalted butter, melted and cooled

2 teaspoons grated orange zest

1 teaspoon grated lemon zest

½ teaspoon vanilla extract

3 or 4 quarter-size pieces of crystallized ginger, coarsely chopped (optional)

confectioners' sugar, for dusting

Adjust oven rack to center position and preheat oven to 350°F. Evenly space six 1- to 1¼-cup ramekins in a large roasting pan.

In a bowl, whisk together 1 cup of sugar, flour, and salt. Add milk, egg yolks, orange juice, lemon juice, melted butter, orange zest, lemon zest, and vanilla and whisk to blend. The batter will be thin.

Using an electric hand or stand mixer on medium speed, beat egg whites until frothy. Gradually add remaining ¼ cup of sugar, increasing mixer speed to high and beating until whites form peaks that droop slightly when beaters are raised.

Fold one-third of the beaten whites into batter. Then fold the remaining whites into batter until well blended. Divide batter evenly among ramekins (they will be about three-quarters full). Top with crystallized ginger (if using).

Pour very hot tap water into roasting pan to come almost halfway up sides of ramekins. Carefully place roasting pan in oven and bake for 40 minutes, or until cakes are puffed and golden brown. Using a slotted spatula, transfer ramekins to a cooling rack for at least 30 minutes. Dust with confectioners' sugar. Serve warm, cold, or at room temperature.

Makes 6 servings.

Cranberry Beet Cake With Orange Walnut Glaze

This cake's pale pink hue makes it a welcome addition to any holiday table. You can cook the beets in your preferred manner—roasting, boiling, even pickling—before using them in this cake.

CAKE:

1¼ cups dried sweetened cranberries

2½ cups all-purpose flour

1½ teaspoons baking powder

1 teaspoon baking soda

1 teaspoon ground cinnamon

¾ teaspoon salt

½ teaspoon ground nutmeg

2¼ cups sugar, divided

1 pound cooked beets, drained and peeled

4 eggs, at room temperature

¾ cup (1½ sticks) unsalted butter, softened

¼ cup vegetable oil

2 teaspoons grated orange zest

2 teaspoons grated lemon zest

2 teaspoons vanilla extract

½ cup buttermilk

GLAZE:

2½ cups confectioners' sugar

2 teaspoons grated orange zest

¼ cup fresh orange juice

1 tablespoon lemon juice

1½ tablespoons unsalted butter, melted

¼ teaspoon vanilla extract

1 cup finely chopped walnuts, for topping

For cake: Adjust oven rack to center position and preheat oven to 350°F. Butter and lightly flour a 10-inch Bundt pan, knocking out excess flour.

Put cranberries into a bowl and add hot water to cover. Set aside.

In a separate bowl, sift together flour, baking powder, baking soda, cinnamon, salt, and nutmeg. Set aside.

In a food processor, combine 1 cup sugar and beets. Process for about 30 seconds, until mixture forms a purée, stopping to scrape down the sides of the bowl once or twice. Set aside.

Using an electric hand or stand mixer, combine remaining 1¼ cups sugar with eggs, butter, and vegetable oil and mix on medium-high for 2 to 3 minutes, or until light and airy. Blend in beet purée. Add orange zest, lemon zest, and vanilla and mix briefly. Add half of dry mixture, then all of buttermilk, then remaining dry mixture, mixing on low after each addition. Drain cranberries and fold into batter. Scrape batter into prepared pan, spreading evenly. Bake for 50 minutes. When done, cake will pull away slightly from sides of pan, and a toothpick inserted into the center will come out clean. Cool cake in pan for 15 minutes, then invert onto a large serving plate and continue to cool. Glaze cake while still warm.

For glaze: Sift confectioners' sugar into a bowl. Add orange zest, orange juice, and lemon juice and whisk to blend. Add melted butter and vanilla and whisk. Glaze should be thick enough to coat cake without running off. If too thick, thin by adding more orange juice, by the half-teaspoon, until it reaches desired consistency. Spoon half of glaze over cake. Sprinkle with walnuts, then cover with remaining glaze.

Makes 16 servings.

FUN FACTS:
• In colonial times, beet dye was used to add color to cake icing and to make pink pancakes.

• Today, beet dye is sometimes used in lemonade, tomato sauce on frozen pizzas, and the ink that butchers use to label meat.

• During World War II, beets proved to be the vegetable that dehydrated the best for use as a ration.

• In 1975, when the *Apollo 18* spacecraft and the Soviet Union's *Soyuz 19* linked up in space, the cosmonauts served the astronauts beet soup squeezed from tubes.

• In Australia, pickled beets—not cucumber pickles—are served on hamburgers.

Bacon Maple Cream Pie

This silky cream pie is full of maple goodness with a scattering of crispy bacon on top. What a perfect combination! Be sure to blind-bake the crust so that it holds its shape and doesn't get soggy once filled.

Basic Pie Pastry (recipe on page 185)

FILLING:

2¼ cups whole milk

2 cups maple syrup,
    preferably grade B

3 egg yolks

½ cup all-purpose flour

3 tablespoons cornstarch

2 teaspoons vanilla extract

TOPPING:

1¼ cups heavy cream, chilled

1 tablespoon sugar

½ teaspoon vanilla extract

4 slices thick-cut bacon

¼ cup maple syrup

1 teaspoon Dijon-style mustard

freshly ground black pepper, to taste

For crust: Preheat oven to 425°F.

Roll chilled dough into a 13-inch circle and line a 9½-inch deep-dish pie plate with it, forming the overhanging dough into an upstanding rim. Line dough in pie plate with foil or parchment paper, then add pie weights (or another pie dish if you don't have pie weights). Blind-bake crust for 15 minutes. Remove pie weights and foil or parchment and return to oven for 5 to 7 more minutes. Cool completely on a rack before filling.

For filling: In a saucepan over low heat, whisk together milk, maple syrup, and egg yolks.

In a bowl, sift together flour and cornstarch. Gradually whisk flour mixture into milk mixture. Stir in vanilla. Increase heat and bring mixture to a boil, cooking for 8 minutes, or until mixture is very thick, stirring constantly. Pour into prepared crust. Refrigerate.

For topping: In a bowl, whip cream with sugar and vanilla. Spread over chilled pie. Refrigerate.

Preheat oven to 375°F. Line a rimmed baking sheet with aluminum foil. Set a cooling rack on foil, and arrange bacon slices across rack in rows, not overlapping.

In a bowl, whisk together maple syrup and mustard. Generously spoon mustard mixture over bacon. Bake for 12 to 15 minutes. Turn over bacon slices and baste again. Bake for 5 to 10 minutes more, or until bacon reaches desired crispness. Remove from oven and sprinkle with freshly ground black pepper. Set aside for 5 minutes. Coarsely chop bacon and sprinkle on top of pie before serving.

Makes 6 to 8 servings.

Basic Recipes

Three-Grain Butter Pastry

Oats and cornmeal give this crust a grainy chew and wholesome appeal. Double the recipe for a double-crust pie. This makes a very leak-resistant dough.

¼ cup old-fashioned rolled oats

¼ cup fine yellow cornmeal

1½ teaspoons sugar

½ teaspoon salt

1 cup all-purpose flour

7 tablespoons cold, unsalted butter, cut into ¼-inch pieces

1 egg yolk beaten with 3 tablespoons cold water

Put oats, cornmeal, sugar, and salt into a food processor and pulse to make a gritty meal. Add flour and pulse to mix. Scatter butter over dry mixture and pulse five or six times, until butter is cut into pieces the size of split peas.

Sprinkle egg mixture over flour mixture in processor. Pulse just until mixture starts to form clumpy crumbs. Do not overprocess.

Transfer crumbs to a large bowl. Pack dough together, as you would a snowball, but don't overdo it. Place dough on a piece of plastic wrap and flatten into a ¾-inch-thick disk. Wrap in plastic wrap and refrigerate for 1 to 1½ hours before rolling. The dough should be slightly pliable, not rock-hard, when you roll it.

Makes enough pastry for one 9½-inch deep-dish pie shell.

Food Processor Tart Dough

This simple tart dough recipe will produce a tender, flaky crust—guaranteed!

1 cup (2 sticks) cold, unsalted butter, cut into ½-inch cubes

2 cups all-purpose flour

¾ teaspoon salt

1 egg beaten with ¼ cup ice-cold water

Chill butter in the freezer for 15 minutes.

Put flour and salt into a food processor and pulse four or five times to mix. Scatter chilled butter on top. Pulse 8 to 10 times more, in 1-second-long bursts, to break butter into very small pieces. Using the feed tube, add egg mixture in an 8- to 10-second-long stream, while pulsing. Continue to pulse until dough forms large, clumpy crumbs.

Turn dough out onto a lightly floured work surface and pack it into a ball. Gently knead once or twice, then flatten into a ½-inch-thick disk. Wrap in plastic wrap and refrigerate for 1 to 2 hours before rolling.

Makes enough pastry for one large tart or one 9-inch double crust.

Basic Pie Pastry

If you haven't yet found your favorite pie dough, try this mistakeproof version. For a two-crust pie, make it twice, rather than doubling the recipe.

1½ cups all-purpose flour

1 tablespoon sugar

1 teaspoon salt

8 tablespoons (1 stick) cold butter, cut into pieces

¼ cup cold water

Put flour, sugar, and salt into a food processor and pulse four or five times to mix. Scatter butter on top. Process for 8 seconds more. Add cold water all at once and process for 6 to 8 seconds, or just until crumbs form. Stop before dough clumps on blade.

Turn mixture out onto wax paper and gather into a smooth ball. Knead once or twice. Chill for 30 minutes to 1 hour before rolling out.

Makes one 9- to 10-inch crust.

Pizza Dough

This is a basic pizza dough recipe to use whenever you're craving homemade pizza. Use it as a vehicle for your favorite seasonal toppings, or try it with the two pizza recipes featured in this book (pages 30 and 125).

1¼ cups lukewarm water (105° to 115°F)

½ teaspoon sugar

1 package (2¼ teaspoons) active dry yeast

3½ cups all-purpose flour, divided

1½ tablespoons olive oil

1½ teaspoons salt

To make the dough by hand: In a bowl, combine water and sugar, then sprinkle with yeast. Set aside for 5 minutes.

To the bowl with the yeast, add 2 cups of flour, 1 cup at a time, and mix well with a wooden spoon. After the second cup, beat briskly 100 times. Wrap dough in plastic and set aside for 10 minutes. Lightly flour a clean work surface.

Remove plastic wrap and add oil, salt, and remaining 1½ cups of flour, ½ cup at a time, beating well after each addition, until dough forms a ball. Turn dough out onto prepared work surface. Knead with floured hands for 8 to 10 minutes, or until dough is supple and springy, adding more flour as necessary to keep dough from sticking to your hands and work surface. Follow Finishing Steps below.

To make the dough using a food processor: This method is suitable for a processor with a 10- to 12-cup capacity and a metal cutting blade. Reduce the amount of water to 1 cup plus 2 tablespoons and put it into a 2-cup measure. Add sugar, then sprinkle with yeast. Set aside for 5 minutes. Add oil and stir to blend.

Put flour and salt into food processor and pulse to mix. Stir sugar and yeast mixture in measuring cup and, using the feed tube on the processor, pour in liquid in a 10- to 12-second-long stream, with processor running. When mixture forms a dough ball that rides above the blade, process (or knead) for 20 to 30 seconds more.

Turn dough out onto a lightly floured work surface and knead with floured hands for 30 seconds. Follow Finishing Steps on opposite page.

Finishing Steps: Lightly oil a large bowl. Place
dough into bowl, rotating to coat surface of dough
with oil. Cover bowl with plastic wrap and set aside to
rise in a warm, draft-free spot for 45 to 60 minutes,
or until doubled in bulk.

*Makes enough dough for 2 large
 or 4 individual-size crusts.*

Index

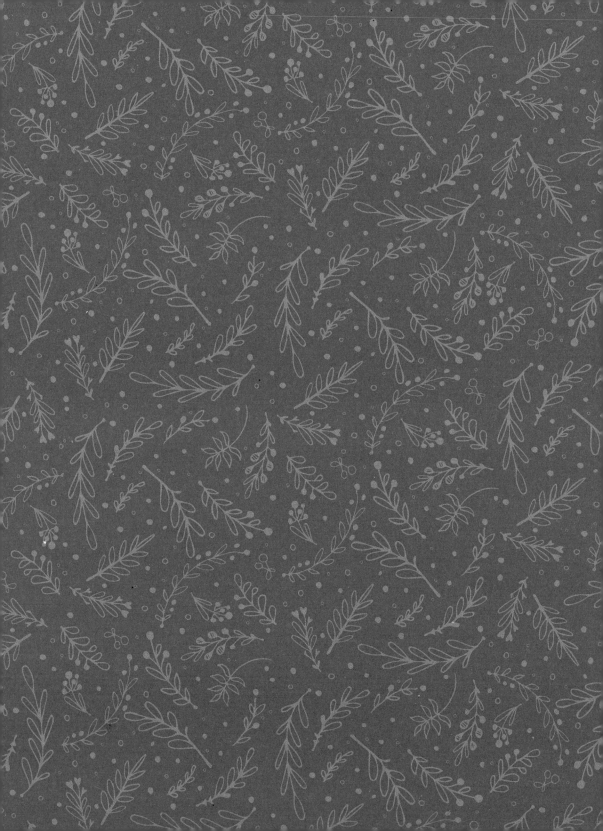